i

THE SOBER VEGAN

Sunshine to Soulshine, becoming healthy one year at a time

Janna Clark

Dear Reader,

This book has been written by me. This is not a polished or synthetic version of my voice. It's the actual work of Janna Clark. It comes from my heart to yours. The information in this book is not meant to replace a qualified therapist.

This book is dedicated to Jordan & Dylan

"to Serious and back and even more."

Table of Contents

ALICE & CARL   JEAN & DALE

    ANN   LYLE   FRAN & THOMAS

SEAN   JANNA   CHAD   TOM   ED

          └──── JORDAN   DYLAN ────┘

Introduction

My journey from child alcoholic and control freak to adult sober vegan has been motivated by pain and freedom. Alcohol, negative thinking, and junk food fueled my disease and wreaked havoc on my body. God was an entity I blamed for my pain and suffering. My biggest challenge was how to change my inner thoughts, my beliefs, and my behaviors.

When I was 19, my life would be changed forever due to a drunk driving accident. I found a mentor, a Higher Power Tree, and chose a word or a phrase to heal my life each year for the past three decades. Eventually, I learned to nurture my mind with information, my body with food, and my spirit with prayer and meditation. Then, the real miracle happened, and I learned to love myself.

This book will take you through my life, year by year, and teach you the simple approach I took to attach to myself and live a congruent life. I used italicized words to represent my inner critical voice and the healthy, nurturing voice I developed to grow, heal, and attach to myself. My experiences, approach to sobriety, and healthy habits are easy to follow, and anyone can do it.

The names of many people in my story have been changed to protect their anonymity.

May this book heal your heart as the tour through my life shines brightly on your soul.

Ready? Here we go!

Chapter One
Family

I was born on April 19, 1972. That makes me an Aries, a fire sign. I am a natural leader, creative, ambitious, brave, energetic, honest, organized, strong-willed, and impulsive. I am also tenacious, passionate, thoughtful, and curious. My parents were Ann and Lyle. Together, they had three children: Sean, Janna, and Chad. We all looked alike, with light blue eyes, high cheekbones, light skin, and brown hair. My brothers look alike, but Sean has more of the Nordic Viking genes with his large muscles, intense stare, and thicker build. Chad looks like the Germans with his sinewy muscles and lanky body.

My parents both grew up in rural communities. Mom was from Nebraska, and Dad was from Minnesota. They both liked watching movies, listening to music, dancing, remodeling homes, playing cards, and drinking. I had an Uncle Gary on each side of the family tree.

My mother's family was large. She had three older siblings, each of whom had four or five children. My memories of my maternal grandparents, Alice and Carl, were loving, attentive, and precious.

My dad's family was small. He had one older brother, Gary, who had two children. I have very few memories of Grandma Jean and Grandpa Dale.

My mother was a strong, brilliant, stoic German woman. She was the last born, and her birth was a miracle. My Grandma Alice lost a child prior to my mom being born. Then, during her pregnancy with my mom, she slipped off a low rung of a ladder and lost much of the amniotic fluid to a tiny leak.

Despite the dry birth, Mom was born healthy and perfect. She grew up on a farm. She loved to climb trees, read books, and sing when she was young. She played the alto saxophone and drove a Volkswagen Bug during high school. She was born in '46 and graduated in '64. She received a certificate from a secretarial college in Denver. She was a single mother in the '80s. She started and owned her own Property Management Company and bought a second-generation Apple computer to run her business. She loved research, traveling, gameshows, learning tech, and time with family. She had a powerful energy that was disturbing and enlightening, depending on how she used it. She felt criticized and abandoned by her parents. This caused post-traumatic stress disorder (PTSD). She was the best mom she could be. My mom and I enjoyed many activities together. We traveled, played cards, read books, put together puzzles, went shopping, and she was my best friend when I was older. I admired her intelligence, strength, and loyalty. She celebrated her sobriety each year on May 22.

My father was French Canadian-Norwegian, tall, organized, funny, playful, and charismatic. He was born in a tiny town in Minnesota. His nickname was Beaver, which he hated. His mom and dad didn't get along, and he grew up with constant stress and discord. His mother was highly critical. His parents divorced, but I am unsure how old my dad was when they separated. He was an excellent basketball player. His parents believed he was skilled enough to obtain a college scholarship. They moved "to the city" to increase his chances, and he was awarded a scholarship and briefly played basketball for a college. Then, he was injured and drafted. Dad served in the Navy as a corpsman and worked in a hospital. His job was caring for patients with lost limbs. He wrapped, rewrapped, and cleaned their stumps. He only talked about it to my mom, brothers, and me once. He loved smoking, drinking beer, gambling, watching hockey, dancing, playing cards, and fishing. Dad called me Sunshine and loved my singing voice. He was there for me the best he could be. We shared some great traits. I am neat and tidy, laugh like him, and have his hands. I admired his joy, energy, and how he could charm a room full of people. He never sustained any sobriety. He had PTSD from his childhood and the Vietnam War.

On their first date, my mother hated my dad. She worked with Uncle Gary, my dad's brother; they worked together at a bank in Denver. She went out with my dad as a favor to Uncle Gary. My dad called the next day and said, "I don't know anyone else; can we please go out again?" She agreed, and they had a much better second date. After a brief courtship, they were married, and the rest is my history.

I was born in a small town in Northern Colorado. My mom told me she was angry at the doctor and yelled at him the exact moment I was born. The Doctor had forced her to have a saddle block, and she was angry. She said, "I was screaming at that damn Doctor the moment you were born." This maybe wasn't the best way to welcome me into the world. My mom was a force when she was triggered or feeling intense emotions. I grew up hearing this story, "You were the ugliest baby I ever saw. Your nose and chin were touching from being so squished up inside. However, the next day, you were beautiful." I believed I was ugly, unlovable, and broken. I felt deep shame from these stories.

When I was about three or four, I would go to bed in our small Colorado ranch home. When I heard the intro for Johnny Carson, I'd wake up. I'd sneak out of bed, creep silently to the wall, and peek around the corner to ensure my mom wasn't awake. I'd come out and climb onto my dad's lap. This was my favorite place. He was big, warm, and soft. I loved how he wrapped his arms around me. I felt loved and safe. We'd be watching Johnny Carson together. He was drinking beer, and so was I. I experienced a wonderful, relaxed, fuzzy, spinning feeling if I drank enough of it. I was not too fond of the taste, but I liked the effect. I remember clearly how much I wanted to be like my dad and experience the relaxed, spinning feeling.

Chapter Two
Iowa

We left Colorado and moved to Iowa when I was four. We had a cream two-story house with a huge picture window in the living room on the upper floor. My bedroom window looked out toward the driveway in front of our house.

My father was a traveling salesman and was no longer home as much. My mom was able to stay home, and she ran a daycare at our house. I remember looking out my bedroom window as my dad drove away when he had to go to work. I felt a horrible emptiness inside, watching him leave. I would want to scream and cry each time he left.

Our home was just up a hill from a creek. There were bugs, turtles, birds, and fireflies to look for and watch. My soul loved having wild animals and nature all around me.

My mom spent much of her time in the kitchen off the living room. She would sing to the radio while preparing dinner. She was most happy when she was in the kitchen. When she made lasagna, she would stand at the Formica counter, cutting the vegetables, draining the noodles, and layering the ingredients for lasagna. It was yummy. The smell would fill the whole house, and my mouth would water. I would stand at the invisible line between the living room and the kitchen with my shoes together and even at the top. I was not allowed to cross that line. These rules were different for my brothers. Her humming was comforting and happy. "Mom, can I look for turtles down by the water?" I asked. "Yes, if Sean goes too and keeps an eye on you."

Sean was three years older than me. My Pink Bink security blanket was in my arms, and we would set off for the creek. "Go over there and play," Sean said with a scowl.

The water changed levels on the banks and often moved very fast. On this day, it was up to the dirt lip and moving like a snake in pursuit of prey. The air was cold and damp on my skin and clothes. My eyes would be searching for life.

"Look! There's a turtle!"

Sean would run over, "Don't move, or you'll scare it. Go get me a stick." When the streetlights came on, we had to be home. If we weren't, mom would yell, "Sean, Janna, get home NOW!" All the neighbors would hear her when she screamed for us, and I felt a heat in my chest and cheeks.

My Siamese cat, Tigger, would bring me dead mice and birds and put them in the middle of the front stoop. "Tigger! Gross! Bad kitty." I would shame her. My mom would say, "Janna, this is nature, animals eat each other, and that's life." I thought it was cruel and gross. Some inner values believed eating animals was wrong, even for my cat. I was young enough not to connect what I was eating with animals, though.

One morning, Tigger woke me up with her strange yowling. I got out of bed and ran to my parents' room. My feet together, I stared into the room. I was nervous about waking up my mom. I thought she would yell at me. Quietly, "Mom," nothing. My mind was scattered and frantic. *Something's wrong with my cat.* I thought. This time, a little louder. "Mom." tick tick tick. I could hear the large clock on the nearby wall. "Mom!" I said as loud as

I thought I could. "What!?" She responded, annoyed. "It's Tigger."

She was in labor. Mom found a big box and cut out the front in a U shape. We helped Tigger to lie down in there with my Pink Bink. Then we put her in the closet, where it was dark and protected. I stayed with her all night.

In the morning, my mother put her on a table in the box. My mother wanted all the kids to learn about the cycle of life, so she invited all the kids from the neighborhood to watch when the kittens were born. I wanted it to be a more private event. I was not happy to have all those kids watching Tigger have her babies. However, I was not consulted. Tigger had six kittens during the day. When it was over, we found clean towels and made the box clean, soft, and warm for Tigger and her kittens. That night, again, I laid my head next to the box in the closet. I felt the hard, cold tile under me. I heard the kittens moving around in the box. I remember being fascinated by the kitten's little faces and closed eyes. I didn't understand how they could find food if they weren't able to see, and I was worried for them.

There was a corner of my blanket I could hold near my face, and that is where I slept, so I could be there if they needed me. I desperately wanted to be there when their eyes opened, too.

"Janna! You leave those kittens alone." My mother scolded. I tried not to touch them too much. While I was watching them, they moved their little heads around and seemed like they couldn't find the milk. "Come on, little kitty, I'll help you." It was such a joy to have those kittens around. I convinced my mom to let me keep the black kitten with a dash of white on her chest. I named her Pepper.

A few months after she had the kittens, Tigger went out and never came home. My mom told me it was expected for an animal to go away when ready to die. My mother had a very farm-oriented belief about animals. She wasn't open to my tender, young ideas either.

"When they die, it's just their time," she said.

Her way of dealing with my soft-feeling heart seemed cold and harsh to me. There was no empathy or talking about my thoughts and feelings.

The family also had a golden retriever named Geiser at the time. Over the years, I loved and cared for guinea pigs, fish, hamsters, birds, cats, and dogs. I spent infinite hours watching wild animals and observing their surroundings and behavior.

When an adult asked, "What do you want to be when you grow up?" I always answered confidently and proudly, "A veterinarian!"

I saw some people using sign language on TV to speak with animals, including dogs, cats, birds, gorillas, chimpanzees, and dolphins. This stimulated my imagination and validated my belief that animals communicate with their eyes, body language, and hands if they were primates. When a show was on about animals, my eyes were glued to the television.

When my dad was home, he crawled around on the living room carpet and wrestled with us. All three of us would climb on his back and roll around on the carpet with him. He would pretend to become a monster, holler, and chase my older brother and me around the house. My mom would grab Chad and keep him safe.

"I am a monster coming to get you."

My heart would start pounding, and my legs felt heavy, like they didn't want to move. This play was fun and exciting, but it was too scary, and my mind was pulsing. I felt hot tears in my eyes. *I don't like to be scared, but Dad's playing with me, so I should play. Mom is protecting Chad and squirms away from me when I come by her; Chad is more valuable.*

We had stairs in the middle of the house. I would sit high up on the stairs where I could see everyone coming and be hidden. I heard my dad yell, "Roar!" I would hear Sean scream. *He will be looking for me next.* My body felt light. Sometimes, I'd float up toward the ceiling. I could see my arms around my legs, and I was scrunched up on one step, trying to be invisible. My head was resting on my knees, and my eyes were closed. *I am safe up here until the game is over.*

I could hear Dad coming around the corner to scare me. "There's my Sunshine," he said in a quiet voice. "You found me," I replied with a grin. The game was finally over, and I jumped off the steps into his arms. I put my arms around his neck. I felt safe and relieved.

"Is it ice cream time?" He said as he looked into my eyes. "Yes!" I shouted. My dad laughed, and we went hunting for ice cream together. I was allowed in the kitchen with my dad.

I loved the attention from my dad, even though I hated the feeling of being afraid. I'd choose to get involved with the excitement of the game so I could be with him. Fear and excitement were blurred together in my mind. Both made my heart pound and my head buzz.

Chapter Three
Kindergarten

Halfway through my kindergarten year, we moved to North Dakota. Our first house in North Dakota was a three-bedroom red house. It was located a few blocks away from the school.

One year, it had snowed constantly for days, and the snow-plowed path between the school and home was over my head. Sean was charged with getting me home from school. "Keep up, Janna," Sean said and rolled his eyes at me. He always scolded me.

My dad was gone even more than in Iowa, and my mom didn't hum or sing when she was in the kitchen anymore. I still wasn't allowed to go into the kitchen when she was cooking, and I saw my mom become more intense and angrier more often.

I'd stand at the invisible line and ask, "Mom, when will Dad be home?"

"I have no idea; now go to your room. I'll call you when dinner is ready."

When my dad arrived home, I would hear him call my name, "Janna, supper is ready."

"Daaaaad!" I shouted as I ran down the hallway and jumped into his arms. "Hey, Sunshine." He would say while he hugged me. My dad carried me to the table and set me on a chair. He smelled like beer and cigarettes. There was a flowery smell too, but I didn't know what it was.

My brothers would already be sitting at the table, and my mom would still be in the kitchen. The air felt tense, and my mother banged pots and pans on the countertop. She'd walk to the table and set the dishes down hard.

"Whoa there, Ann, be careful, or you'll break something, hahaha." my dad would joke. "I'd like to break something over your head." My mom retorted under her breath.

"Oh Ann, you don't mean that; you love me. Come here and give me a smooch, hahaha." My father would grab my mom's butt and laugh some more. The air felt thick and tense. I watched my mom's body getting stiffer, and her movements became sharper. I'd laugh when my dad did, and my mom would glare at me so I'd stop. I felt heat move up from my stomach to my face. We'd eat dinner with this mockery from my dad and dangerous anger from my mom repeatedly for years. It was the dance happening between my parents. I didn't understand how it had affected me for years. It only happened on the nights my dad came home for dinner. As time moved forward, he came home less and less. I felt more alone and sadder on the nights he wasn't home.

When my dad didn't come home, I witnessed another pattern. She'd call Big Daddy's to check if he was there. "Hi, this is Ann. Is Lyle there?" She rolled her eyes. "Well, tell him we are eating dinner now." Click. On these nights, she was quiet. There were butterflies in my stomach. *I wish I could go and be with Dad.*

One night, when I was about six years old, I was intentionally drinking my dad's beer to get the spinning feeling. My dad shook the can, and I could hear the 'tink-tink' of the tab top hitting the sides of the empty can. He realized his beer was gone. He said, "Where's my beer?"

"I drank it, Dad," I say nervously. Then he laughed with a huge grin and squeezed me tight while he looked at me. I have been looking for that approval and joy on the faces of men ever since. It was pride. It was attention. It was love.

I had the most horrible, painful earaches when I was young. I would get an earache to the point of breaking my eardrum. The pain would stop when my eardrum broke. It was the only time I felt cared for by my mother.

I read some research years ago about the correlation between parents who smoke cigarettes around children and earaches. Both of my parents smoked in the house. I think this, along with small inner ear canals and overactive candida or yeast in my body, caused my repeated earaches.

When my mom brought me to the doctor, he said, "Ann, Janna needs tubes to try to stop the earaches. We are concerned that the scar tissue will damage her hearing."

In preparation for surgery, my mom asked, "Janna, what would you like to eat for dinner tomorrow night? You can have chili or tiny gravy hamburgers and potatoes. I don't have the time to make lasagna."

"Can we have potatoes with tiny burgers?" I asked. They were one of my favorite meals.

When we lived in North Dakota, we ate Red River Valley potatoes. They were the most delectable potatoes on Earth. I still think of them each time I eat potatoes. My Grandpa Carl believed they were delicious because of the dark, rich soil in North Dakota. He loved those red potatoes, too!

"Do you want to have lefsa with cinnamon sugar for dessert?" My mom asked. "Yes!" I shouted with a little jump in the air.

Lefse (Pronounced: lef-sa) looked like a mix between a crepe and a tortilla. They are made from potatoes.

I would get one out of the fridge and lay it on the coil of the electric stove until the coil started to smoke. It was meant to be warm, but it would have small burn spots on it most of the time. Then, I would rip it off the burner and plop it on a plate. I was trying not to burn myself on the hot coil. Mom would add butter and cinnamon sugar, roll it up, and they were ready to eat. When lefse was homemade from Red River Valley potatoes, it was delicious. Hopefully, someday, I will eat them vegan and gluten-free. Uffda!

The Doctor had decided I needed to have tubes put in my ears; it was terrifying. I was taken to the big, sterile, white hospital. My tiny body was on this huge, cold, hard metal bed. I was told to put on a gown with nothing to cover my back, and I was freezing. My parents were not with me as the nurse took me to the operating room.

"Breathe deeply and count to ten." the nurse instructed as she covered my face. The smell of plastic and some kind of strong cleaner filled my nose. *I don't like that smell.* "One," was all I said.

The next memory was someone saying my name and pushing me hard. "Janna! Wake up! Come on, Janna, open your eyes!" A long, bright light in a strange ceiling came into view. The light hurt my eyes. *I am so dizzy.* I blinked slowly.

I don't like this kind of dizzy. I looked over at the unfamiliar woman. *I want to stay asleep.*

"Hi Janna; I am glad you woke up. You scared me."

"Where is my dad?" I whisper groggily. "I don't know, but someone will be here soon." *My stomach hurts, and I am cold. I am here all alone.* Then I floated up. I saw a row of empty beds around me, and the nurse was standing next to mine. My body is tiny compared to the bed.

I am safe, I think. The nurse covered my body with a warm blanket, and I sunk back into my body. Then I fell asleep again.

The tubes did help, and I outgrew earaches for the most part as a teenager.

My parents built a big new house on some land a few blocks from our old house. In this house, my mom had a formal living room with white carpet and two white wing-backed chairs. They were positioned in front of the bay window. On the opposite wall was a large hutch containing the eight-track, record player, and radio. My dad wired speakers into all the rooms so music could be heard in the house.

I knew all the words to *The Stranger* album by Billy Joel and *The Grease* soundtrack. Whenever the radio was on, I'd sing. If I weren't singing, I would be talking. This irritated my mom.

On the way to school, Mom always played the radio. I'd sing and talk. "Shut up!" My mom screamed while driving down the road. My body froze. My heart started to pound hard in my chest and ears, my head felt full, and a knot formed in my stomach. *Don't cry. You'll make mom more angry,* I told myself.

Sean looked back from the front seat. He'd shake his head back and forth, and he'd scowl at me. My chest flushed with heat. I looked down at my shoes and held my breath. *You made mom mad,* I thought. Silent, hot tears would run down my cheeks.

Don't talk, be quiet, and just shut up! You are bothering everyone. Don't be happy. It hurts your family. I shamed myself.

My Grandpa Dale had a favorite lake with good camping and fishing. Sometimes, he would bring us to fish from his boat. My mom would prepare several meals for the trip. She'd make my most memorable foods: eggs and bacon, chili, and hobo dinners. All of these were our camping foods.

My mom's chili was wonderful. It had kidney, white, and pinto beans, ground beef, crushed tomatoes, chili powder, onions, and garlic. She cooked it all day in a crockpot. Then used an empty vanilla ice cream container, gallon-sized, and put it in the freezer out in the garage. We ate it with oyster crackers or buttered bread. Hobo dinners were made with onions, carrots, and potatoes peeled and cut into large pieces. The Hobo dinners were generally prepared at the campground with our help. The vegetables were piled on a rectangle of tin foil. Then, tablespoon-sized butter hunks from a cube of butter were generously placed on top of the veggies. Raw ground beef chunks were added, and Lawry's Seasoning was sprinkled generously over the top. We rolled up the tinfoil to make a pouch and threw it on the grill. The pouch was placed on the metal grill over the fire. She used her Coleman stove for eggs and bacon at breakfast, and the frozen chili was heated up in a large pot for lunch. She'd also make hotdish sometimes when it was going to be colder than usual outside.

It was extremely cold in North Dakota in the fall and wintertime. She called hotdish "hockey food." I believe hotdish is also called goulash. It was made with onions, ground hamburger meat, pasta, corn, tomato sauce, and spices.

While fishing in our red Lund outboard boat, if we caught northern or walleye, Dad would clean them, and we'd have fresh fish with freshly squeezed lemon, herbs, and butter.

"Janna, go ask your dad how much longer until he is ready with the fish."

"Okay, Mom!" I would run from the campsite to the fish house. Then, about nine feet away, my feet would slow. My nose would sniff slowly. If it didn't smell horrible, I'd move closer.

Fish houses were tiny sheds full of giant buzzing flies. The floors were covered in crates with dark, dried blood and fisheyes stuck between the wood slates. The wooden cutting blocks had rotten fish meat, slime, and scales covering them, and the smell made me gag. It was a total freak show. *Gross!* As I approached, I would call out. "Dad, mom wants to know how much longer?"

"Tell your mother I will be about ten more minutes." *Dad must be irritated at Mom,* I thought. I knew this when he called her "your mother." Mom and Dad both did this; when they were irritated or angry with the other parent, they'd identify them as belonging to us and say "YOUR."

Before I can run away, my father peeks his head around the wall of the fish house. "Hey, Janna, this is the walleye you caught; you need to come and flay it?"

Dad was very tidy; he would have a bucket of clean water, Dawn dish soap, and a wooden-handled scrub brush. He cleaned the wood thoroughly before, during, and after his task. He had a special knife designed for this job, which was stored in a leather pouch.

"Okay," I said. My dad hands me his special knife. He puts his hand over mine to show me how to hold it. "Put it behind the gill and push down at an angle until you feel the bones." I can feel the knife cutting into the flesh of the fish. I see the eye bulge, and a trickle of blood runs down the limp body. My stomach lurches. *This is gross. The poor fish, I took its life.* I did some of the job, but my dad could see I was nauseated and didn't want to cut up this animal, so he rescued me. "Go tell mom I'm almost done." I run from that hut of horrors as fast as I can.

At dinner time, we were all sitting in our folding camping chairs. My feet didn't touch the ground, and I liked swinging them back and forth. "Janna, eat the fish slowly. It still has all the little bones in it, and it could choke you." *Choke me? Like I could die? Scary!*

I liked the taste of the fish, but dealing with the bones irritated me, and I often didn't eat much of it. I also felt uncomfortable knowing this animal was alive, swimming along just a few hours ago. I didn't like knowing I had taken a life. It seemed unnecessary. I felt conflicted by how I felt about animals and the fact I was eating them.

Chapter Four
Trust Issues

I went to school in a red brick ranch-style school. There were exit doors on the interior and exterior of the building with windows on the outside wall.

I wanted my schoolwork to be perfect, so I worked slowly at a careful pace. Mrs. Johnson, my first-grade teacher, communicated in a confusing and difficult way for me to understand. She came over to me one day and said, "If you don't get your work done, then you'll need to stay in at recess and work," her intention was to motivate me to speed up my pace. *Oh good, I will get more time to do my work perfectly.* I thought.

I had a sharp, focused mind and a strong work ethic. I liked doing the work, and my ambition fueled my desire to be perfect. I was willing to miss recess to get a star on my paper. Going out to recess was fraught with uncomfortable dilemmas I didn't know how to navigate. Mrs. Johnson didn't understand my priorities and motives.

"Janna, what are you doing here? Are you still working?" Mrs. Johnson said in an annoyed tone of voice.

"I am just finishing my work."

"Well, just go outside and play."

"I'm not done," I exclaim with disbelief.

"Just give it to me and go outside," she said dismissively.

I stood up slowly and went outside, feeling sluggish with disappointment and betrayal. *She lied to me. She said I could stay in and do my work.* I felt confused.

Then, finally, one day, Mrs. Johnson handed back graded papers, and I was excited about getting a star on my worksheet. *I reached my goal. I did a good job!* I thought excitedly.

I wanted to tell someone about my success, so I talked to the girl sitting next to me, "I got a star. How did you do?" She looked at my page and replied, "I didn't do this one." *What? Why did I do different work? Mrs. Johnson doesn't like me, that's why.* I tried to puzzle it out. *The teacher must be giving me extra work. If I could do the page perfectly, I'd get less work, and she would let me move on. I do not want additional work; that'd be unfair. Maybe I am not as smart as the other kids.* I think, with a knot forming in my belly.

When I told my mom how upset I was, she called the school to meet with Mrs. Johnson. My desk was in the far-right row near the back of the classroom. The room was empty, aside from Mrs. Johnson and my mother standing in front. My mom was holding Chad on her hip.

They were talking quietly, and I couldn't hear the entire conversation, "At her own pace," my mom said.

"doesn't,"

"if she," and "focus."

Then, I heard my mom laugh with the enemy. My stomach clenched, my ears buzzed, and my bowels were rumbling. *Why is she laughing with this mean woman? I thought she'd help me. She doesn't care about me. I am not smart enough. I am not her favorite child. I'll never be any good at school. I hate them both.* I didn't have the maturity to understand how I was affected by the moment, but I believed I could no longer trust my own mother.

Trust is earned in small quantities over time, like the drips from a faucet and quickly broken like a spilled metal pale of water. I knew my mom loved me because I was her daughter; however, I didn't feel cared for by her. The difference between being loved and being cared for is belonging and connection. My mom didn't take the time to talk to me about their conversation after the meeting. I needed a chance to understand what she learned and what they talked about, ask questions, and accept anything I didn't like. I needed information, comfort, and support. I needed to be cared for. There was no conversation. "Janna, you need to work faster in school, okay?" That was it. *She's on Mrs. Johnson's side and not mine. I am on my own to figure this all out.*

Chapter Five
Abandoned

The summer after first grade, my dad moved out. Again, I wasn't informed about what was happening. My mom put a laundry basket full of my dad's clothes by the front door. "Is Dad going on a trip?" I asked my angry, silent mother.

"No, he's staying somewhere else."

"Where?" I asked.

My mother was silent, and I could feel her intensity. I wanted answers and reassurance. There was only silence as she moved around the house with purpose. *What's happening? Where is Dad going? I want to be with my dad.* I feared losing his time and attention. *Dad will want me to stay with him.* I reassured myself. I was wrong.

Dad moved into a second-floor, two-bedroom apartment across town. I wasn't familiar with this part of town. On a few Friday nights, my brothers and I visited him. Shortly after he moved, he introduced us to Roxy. I looked away and hugged my dad. *I can smell the flowers again.*

My dad thought it was funny when I ignored her. He laughed and then hugged me tightly. I already thought I didn't have enough time with him. *This is mom's fault for being so mean.* I blamed my mom. I felt confused, angry, and hurt. We all watched a movie at his new apartment. I sat on my dad's lap and told Roxy she had to sit on the couch, nowhere near my dad. Again, my dad laughed at my sass, and Roxy sat on the couch with my brothers. I didn't want to feel sad, hurt, and afraid. I was trying to find a solution without any healthy support. Beer helped me let go of my thoughts and feelings, so I'd continue to drink his beer whenever I was with my dad. Then, I could stop thinking and feeling. I could relax.

My mother's behavior during this time was confusing and volatile. She was yelling more and getting angry more, and then suddenly, she became happy and funny. I didn't see it then, but she must've been drinking more, which accounts for her sudden mood swings and volatility in the mornings.

One evening, my mom went out on a date. She'd hired a girl I didn't know to babysit us. The babysitter was sitting in the formal living room with the elegant white curtains and two white wing-back chairs angled around the side table. It was carpeted with a light white soft plush carpet. The kind that leaves lines in it after it's been vacuumed. My mother loved this room. I wasn't allowed to go into this room without permission. The transition between the hardwood and the carpet was the line.

I came down the stairs to see the babysitter sitting on one of the chairs, painting her nails red. My breath stopped as she looked up at me; I watched her spill red fingernail polish on the side table and the chair's cushion. "When my mom comes home, you are going to be in big trouble," I told her. "My mother is going to scream at you."

The babysitter tried to clean it up, but I could see it was permanently on the cushion. I knew my mother was going to freak out. I never dreamed I'd be the one she'd freak out on.

"Janna Nicole! Get your ass downstairs right now!" My mom screamed. I woke up with my heart pounding.

What's wrong? I came, running down the hall from my bedroom. *What happened?* I thought.

"Did you spill red nail polish on my white chairs?"

"No, it was the babysitter, not me," I said. I looked at my mother's furious face and felt chills run down my spine. I saw the wooden spoon in her hand. I had seen her whipping my older brother with this spoon, and I knew what she had planned for me. "I do not believe you!" My mom screamed.

She grabbed my arm and spun my body around. She threw my tiny chest up against her and pinned me to her legs. She started hitting me on the butt with the wooden spoon as hard as possible.

I began to cry, "Stop. Stop. Please stop." When she was done wailing on me, I ran upstairs and closed my bedroom door."

I sat on the floor next to the bed and placed all my stuffed animals around me in a circle. I wanted to feel safe. There was no break in the circle. *They'll protect me from her.* I cried as quietly as I could. I didn't want her to hear me and come into my room. Finally, I floated up to the ceiling and fell asleep. My body would heal, but my heart was wounded deeply. *Why doesn't she believe me?* I felt betrayed and unloved by my mother. *If Dad were here, she wouldn't have done that. Now I am alone.* The metal pale spilled.

I had an excellent, loving teacher named Mrs. Peterson in second grade. I spent two years in second grade with this wonderful, caring teacher. Once again, conversations were happening between the adults about me and decisions made, and I wasn't included. I believe this was an attempt by the adults around me to be supportive. However, it reinforced false beliefs about myself. I believed I was dumb.

I was not paying attention in school. I was mentally busy solving problems; I wanted to think my way out. I didn't realize I had no power or choice. *How could I get more time with my dad? Why do I have to be alive? Why are my brothers more valuable than me?*

I was also no longer interested in doing well in school because I believed I couldn't be successful. My ambition shifted, and so did my attention. I had begun to stare out the window and let my mind wander for hours at a time. I wanted to be outside with the animals.

I will never know if holding me back was the right decision. I have very few memories of my first year. I think it was both good and bad. It was good for me to stay with Mrs. Peterson. I desperately needed her hugs and attention.

"Janna, Good news! You and I are going to have another year together." She explained.

"Am I the only one staying with you?"

"Yes, dear, you and I have a little more work to do, and I am excited to spend more time with you." She emphasized.

I was experiencing such trauma and abandonment from losing my dad, so another year with her seemed like a win to me. However, I didn't want to stay in second grade for another year. It also felt like punishment.

Chapter Six
Hugs

I was better connected to Mrs. Peterson during my second year of second grade. She was a tall, heavyset woman with open arms, bright blue eyes, and a gentle expression. I knew after the previous year I could trust her. She would stand at the back door of her classroom and hug us as we entered her room in the ranch-style brick school.

"Good morning, Janna, and how are you today?" I was greeted at the door.

"I'm fine."

"Oh good, that's a nice big hug, thank you."

Mrs. Peterson would also hug us when we left for the day. I received two needed hugs every school day for two years. What an incredible blessing. Mrs. Peterson taught me to read as I sat at the kidney bean-shaped table in my tiny chair. She had a transparent red plastic toy car. When I pushed it forward on its wheels, the bottom would light up with flashing lights. It reminded me of the Flash Lightning car and song from the Grease album.

She told me, "Periods are stop signs, and commas are yield signs." Then she looked me in the eyes and waited for me to nod. I nodded. "When you see a period, use the car and stop. Take a breath, then start your new sentence. When you see a comma, pause. Then keep reading to learn more." *Breathe long for a period and short for a comma.* "Nice job, sweetheart, you're doing great!" She encouraged.

Mrs. Peterson taught us the golden rule: "Treat others how you would want to be treated. Who knows what that means?"

"Janna."

"It means to be nice to other people," I answered. "Then they will be nice to me, too," I added after her encouraging nod. "That's right!" she said with a smile.

When a student had a birthday, Mrs. Peterson would read *The Birthday Book* by Dr. Suess. She changed the names in the book to her students' names, and I loved to hear her read my name during story time.

"The great birthday bird! And, so far as I know, Katroo is the only place Birthday Birds grow. This bird has a brain. He's most beautifully brained with the brainiest bird-brain that's ever been trained. He was trained by the most splendid Club in the nation, The Katroo Happy Birthday Asso-see-eye-ation. And whether your name is Michelle, Janna, Kim, or Paul When your birthday comes round, he's in charge of it all."

She supported me in important, simple ways. She would crouch down and get me to look into her eyes when she told me something I needed to remember. She smiled at me. She hugged me. She praised me. I will never forget this meaningful connection. She was my security at such a difficult time in my life. There can never be enough Mrs. Petersons in the schools. I had some excellent teachers, and I had some teachers with challenging behaviors. As an adult looking back in simple terms, the difference was shame and support. The good teachers supported, nurtured, and loved me for who I was. They took the time to explain things so I could understand. The teachers with challenging behaviors didn't take the time to communicate clearly, and they used manipulation and shame to try to manage their students. I felt seen, heard, and loved by Mrs. Peterson. *I Am I.*

My mom picked up Sean and me on the last day of school. "Kids, we are moving back home." *What? Where is home? We are home; Dad is here. Dad will want me to stay with him for sure.* I thought. "Where will we go?" I asked. "Home." My mother responded with a smile. I felt numb. *What does this mean?* I wondered. I didn't believe it was true.

My mom, brothers, and I left North Dakota to go to Nebraska. It was a warm sunny day, and Mom's station wagon was packed to the top of the back seats. There was a cage at my feet with Pepper in it; my brother Chad was in the back seat with me, and Sean was sitting up front with Mom. I clearly remember watching out the car's rear window as we drove away from my dad. He was looking at us and waving his hand in the air. I watched his face fall as he turned to walk away. My heart was broken. According to my mom, I said, "I hate you." I don't remember this, but I would guess it's accurate.

We drove from the paved, flat Nebraska highway to the gravel road, and my mom said, "Kids, there it is!" I could see a white house with a green roof in the far-off distance. There were huge trees all around it and a few other buildings. Toward the left side were three tall round metal silos. When we arrived, Grandpa Carl was sitting at the blue kitchen table at the top of three steps, and Grandma Alice was standing in the entryway, ready with hugs for all of us.

Grandpa Carl was a tall, broad-shouldered man. He had long arms and big hands, feet, and ears. He had steel blue eyes and a mostly bald head. He loved being a farmer, adored my grandmother, and was a ruthless businessman. Grandma Alice looked like Betty White, right down to the dimples. She was beautiful inside and out. She was English, Danish, and German. She loved to play cards and was extremely good at it. She also enjoyed quilting, crocheting, and cooking. Loving her family was her life's purpose. She was ready with her arms open and giving us all big, warm, soft hugs. *This feels like Mrs. Peterson's hugs.*

Grandpa stayed in his chair and greeted us with a big smile. Grandma Alice had food ready for us. She was happy and smiling, too. "Hellooooo! How was the trip? Come in, come in. I have supper ready. Are you hungry?" I felt loved.

The farmhouse had a huge picture window where the table sat in the kitchen. This is where we would eat together. We would talk and listen to each other. I learned to play cards there. This is where most of my fondest memories are with family. I always felt warmth and love from my grandparents. It's probably why I value quality time with people.

Living closer to them was good for my soul. We stayed on the farm for the summer, and I learned to watch the wheat on the farm as it grew, then ripened, changed, and was finally ready to be harvested. Grandpa Carl would make comments like, "Well, it's still green in the middle," and "It's starting to look the right color gold." He and I walked into the wheat fields to check if it was ready for the harvest. He kindly guided, "Follow my footsteps as best as you can so we don't damage the wheat."

My reverence and respect for plants started with the teachings of my grandparents. My grandpa didn't use chemicals or pesticides on his wheat. It was safe to walk into a field to check on its ripeness. It was fertile, and some of it would be put aside for next year's planting. The rest would be either stored in round metal bins called silos or sold if the price was higher than at peak harvesting season. Bees were flying around in the fields, and they were alive. Grandpa showed me how to test ripeness using my senses. We would walk to the wettest part of the land, where the ground was softest. Grandpa would break off the head of one wheat stalk, roll it between his fingers to listen for a crunchy sound, and test the dryness. Then, he would squeeze the kernels onto his palm and try to cut through one with his thumbnail. Finally, he would pop them into his mouth and chew them. He could predict when it would be ready for harvest with the accuracy that only comes with years of experience.

I loved this practice. I felt connected to my grandpa, the farm, and the earth. It filled me with love and joy. I tried to always be at Grandpa's side when it was time to check the field.

I spent a month every summer on the farm with my loving grandparents until I was sixteen. They asked my brother Chad and me questions and listened to our answers for hours. They showed me the joy and value of being out in a vast open space with the big blue sky above me. They taught me how to read the clouds and alert them if one was green and looked like it could become a funnel. Nebraska was windy and had tons of flies. They taught me to kill flies with a fly swatter and then clean them up. We did everything together. When I was on the farm with my grandparents, I was not in charge, and I could be a kid. I'm a better person because they were in my life.

Chapter Seven
Colorado

My mom found a job with a property management company in Northern Colorado, so we left the beloved farm and my wonderful grandparents. We moved a few days before school started. We had a fenced yard with tons of shrubbery and a huge locust tree out front. Mom, Chad, and I all had bedrooms on the top floor of the house. Sean had a bedroom in the finished basement.

In Colorado, I noticed that there were lots of bright sunny days and few bugs. I loved looking out at the mountains when I was outside. We lived one block from the elementary school Chad, and I would attend. Sean's middle school was about one and a half miles from the house, and he would have to walk a long way to and from school each day.

My mom had to work full-time, so my eating habits and access to healthy food changed dramatically. Mom had less money and time, which translated to less energy for making home-cooked meals. I ate eggs, sugary cereals with cow's milk, Kraft macaroni and cheese, anything in a can, and bread. Cheap, sugary, processed, accessible foods with a long shelf life. Welcome to The Standard American Diet (SAD).

Sean was mean and angry. He teased me about being stupid; he'd roll his eyes and say, "Ignorance is bliss" when I talked about things. He was physically aggressive toward me often.

There were times he would pin me on the ground and spit in my mouth. Other times, he would use his knees, hold down my arms, and pound his middle knuckle on my chest until it left a red mark. He called it "a cherry." He was a bully, with no one around to stop him. Sean only lived in Colorado for about a year. I was told he missed playing hockey and didn't like the kids in Colorado. He decided to move back to North Dakota to live with our dad. I felt safer at home after he left.

I suffered from anorexia. I felt no desire to eat most of the time. I could go for two weeks without having a bowel movement. I would get dizzy and almost blackout regularly. I had horrible heartburn, but I was too afraid to ask someone what it was. I was a nail-biter and would bite my skin off until it bled, and I hurt myself. I was experiencing horrible gas all the time. When I was involved in something athletic, I would get severe pain in my side and become short of breath. I felt depressed and angry often. I was not comfortable in my body. I lived in a world of control, obsessions, and anxiety. I was perpetually afraid and disconnected. Stress made all my physical symptoms worse.

We had to be responsible for getting to school on time. We had a clock with Roman numerals in the kitchen, and I learned how to tell time on the clock.

In third grade, I met a lifelong friend, Margret. She was a sweet, kind girl with blond–brown hair, big blue eyes, and pretty curls. I loved her smile. After recess, one day, I saw a red-headed girl being mean to her while we were hanging up our coats. The Aries warrior part of my personality was fierce and ready for a battle. I matched the red-headed girl's meanness with my meanness.

Margret and I became friends. I loved going to her house because her mom was always home. She ran a daycare out of their home. There were always people coming and going, including her two older brothers. I could see how everyone was kind to each other. Her mom would cook meals and make snacks. Family, love, and support surrounded Margret. I was jealous of all she had. I felt isolated, alone, and lonely at my house. My mom was always gone and rarely cooked anymore. My older brother didn't care for me. When we would get together, we would sing and laugh for hours. I don't remember all of the things we would laugh about, but I remember some of them still. We laughed a lot.

Thank God for my friends, then and now.

Chapter Eight
Loneliness

In fourth grade, being different from the other kids was noticed, and I was different. Most of the children in my school had a mom and a dad at home. I had no dad, and my mom was rarely home. Most of them were not assuming the role of an adult with the cleaning, cooking, and responsibility I had taken on. None of them were drinking alcohol for the numbing effect.

My mom had started her own property management company, and she was rarely home. I recall some nights when I would wake up and hear *M*A*S*H* on the television downstairs. When I walked down to see her, she would be passed out on the couch. There would be an ashtray on the floor next to her and an empty glass of wine or vodka. Sometimes, a cigarette would burn on the tile floor next to the ashtray.

"Mom! Go to bed." I would say.

Some nights, she would respond, "Yup." Most nights, she didn't respond at all. When she didn't respond, I would check her breathing. She rarely went to bed. I'd shut off the TV, clean up the ashtray, and put the empty glass in the sink. I was afraid she would fall and hurt herself on the glass or cigarettes. Then, I would return to my bedroom and try to fall asleep again.

I didn't realize it then, but alcohol was seriously affecting my mom's life. Which meant it was affecting mine too. I often felt alone and lonely. I missed my dad. I took on responsibility and added control to it. Without any adults there to monitor and guide me, control allowed me to feel safe. My younger brother experienced the consequences of my controlling bossiness. It didn't take long before my mom started sleeping or passing out at her office frequently. Most mornings, I would wake up and check her room. I was constantly looking for evidence of her presence. After school, I'd see a plate and fork in the sink or water in the shower, and I'd know she had come home while we were at school and then left again. If my brother and I needed something, we called her office. She threatened us with a babysitter if we told anyone about being left at home alone. My babysitter experiences were not positive, so I learned what happens at home stays at home.

When mom was home, she was constantly angry and screaming. It felt personal and violent. When she wasn't screaming, it was worse. The violence of her seething silence put chills down my spine. She was miserable and dangerous. I experienced the brunt of her alcoholic resentment and rage. Sean was in North Dakota with Dad, and Chad seemed to be her favorite. He also had quick wit and humor to defuse her sharp criticism. I am not funny.

On the nights when she did come home, I'd listen to how the door closed and the pace and pressure of her walk to gauge her mood. I believed if I did everything perfectly for her, she would like me and care for me. The few times I thought it worked fueled my damaging controlling behavior.

My mom always had a cardboard box of Zinfandel in the fridge. The box had a spout to pour from in the front. I didn't need to be careful about how much I drank because there wasn't a way to see how much was left in the silver bag on the inside of the container.

Fourth grade was when my consistent drinking began. I would come home from school and do all my chores. Then, I'd get a water glass from the cupboard and fill my glass with some wine from the box. I felt grown up. I'd sit in front of the TV eating sugary cereal or mac and cheese and zone out. I let the alcohol work its magic on my feelings of loneliness, sadness, and fear. Television, sugar, and alcohol effectively numbed my head and my heart. The monotony of my life dragged on like this for years. We moved from the house to a rental condo, another rental condo, and finally, a trailer.

Each summer, I would spend a month visiting my grandparents on the farm and then a few weeks to a month at my dad's trailer in North Dakota. While we visited, we didn't see much of my dad. He spent his time at work and then went to the bar. We would spend one weekend camping and fishing. There was always a lot of beer there and unpredictable drunk adults.

It felt like years of the same old thing, hour after hour. Time was a device that marked my misery and loneliness.

I treasured my cat Pepper, my brother Chad, my friend Margret, and my love of singing. My cat was my constant companion. I loved talking to her and snuggling with her. My brother Chad was funny, with his boyish mischief and shiny smile. He and I would make faces at each other in the mirror just to try to make each other laugh. We would memorize commercials and recite them over and over like a skit. To this day, we can repeat commercials word for word. We had all the time in the world for each other.

"Hey Chad," I said in my best southern drawl, like the actors in the commercial.

"Hey, what?" he replied in his drawl. Now, we both knew what came next. "Whatcha got there?"

"That's right." Then, we would both break out in giggles. The more he laughed, the more I laughed. Many of my happy childhood memories have Chad in them.

I enjoyed singing class the most in elementary school. In 5th grade, I tried out for and was accepted into The Children's Choral group. The director was my music teacher; she was a stoic woman, had a serious expression, and was quick and direct if anyone made a mistake. She was a little bit like my mom in that way. She lacked the intensity and edge of my mom, though. The director knew I was a good singer and encouraged me to try out. It was a safe place where I felt accomplished and praised. I found some belonging in this group. Also, my mom liked the idea of me singing, and I was happy to please her.

Eventually, work was more important to my mom than attending my concerts, so I rarely had a ride to and from the performances. I walked miles to the shows and then miles home because I was too embarrassed to ask for a ride and admit I was alone. I would walk out of my way so my teacher and fellow performers wouldn't know. I felt ashamed and alone. I'm grateful I grew up in a small town where walking was safe and easy.

From eight years old until I went to college, I played the part of an adult, caring for my brother, drinking wine, and doing all the household tasks. While I was at school, I was treated like a child. It was incongruent, and I responded by not investing my full effort at school and using anything available to numb and avoid my feelings.

The blessing was the month each summer when my brother Chad and I went to the farm in Nebraska. This was a place I felt supported, nurtured, and safe. I could relax and didn't have to be in control. Grandma cooked for my brother Chad and me.

She would make us three meals a day. We would sit around the table for breakfast, lunch, and dinner while talking and eating. I didn't feel like I was responsible for Chad. I could be his sister. We rode the three-wheeler, swung on the tree swing in the backyard, and helped Grandma with anything she needed.

When Grandpa Carl came in off the tractor in the evening, we would have the square, blue Formica kitchen table set for dinner. Grandma Alice and Grandpa Carl sat and listened to my younger brother and I talk for hours. The conversation moved from the price of wheat to an event in town or the nearby tiny community. Then they would turn to us and ask, "What do you think?" No matter how we responded, they would praise and encourage us, "Oh, that is an interesting thought."

"Janna, what do you think?" It was my turn. Then, follow up with more questions. "What about...?" They modeled manners, respect, and kindness. I felt loved, heard, and valued.

I helped Grandma with her large garden. She gave me the experience of eating fresh spinach, strawberries, tiny carrots, sweet peas, and green onions that we cared for and grew together. She taught me to look for bugs and the natural ways to combat bugs without pesticides.

"Did you know that slugs love beer?"

"Really?"

"Yes, if we put a little bit in this butter container, it will attract them, and they will not eat our plants." *Grandma won't say they'll die because she knows I'll be upset about that.* I thought to myself. "That's cool, grandma." We would check on the food and water the plants every afternoon. It was inspiring to interact with our food and have a hand in growing it. What a glorious connection!

Grandma Alice had read a book about food pairing; she would serve pineapple with beans "to prevent becoming gassy." She told us, "Carrots are good for our eyes, and flax will help with healthy BMs." She was interested in food, nutrition, and cooking. She liked natural things and had a powerful connection with the earth. Grandma Alice was a breath of fresh air.

They taught me the value of hard work and a natural lifestyle. The values they instilled in me are in my soul forever. I still feel closer to them when I am out in nature. Those values were the beginning of my vegan path.

One summer, Chad and I made a trail through the windbreak. A windbreak is a group of strategically planted trees to help block the wind in the plains of Nebraska. Our route went through the windbreak, around the front of the house, by the garage and outbuilding, to the edge of the field, behind the junkyard, and by the Quonset hut. Then, we were back at the entrance to the trees. We rode the red Honda three-wheeler for hours every day after helping Grandma. Grandpa had a gas tank on the farm, so we just pulled up and filled the tank when we ran low on gas. I loved the speed and the air blowing around my body. The three-wheeler was freedom from my troubles and let me play. It was excitement and adrenaline.

One day, I caught sight of a bright orange fox with a tip of white on its tail. It took days of stealthy movements to figure out where the fox lived, but my brother and I found the entrance to its home. It was out behind the junkyard at the edge of a wheat field. That's when I realized there were two of them. The field was not planted yet, so we could ride on the edge to see the foxes. I was so excited.

I watched them every day. I watched them become four and saw the babies peek their heads out. Those foxes could have been afraid of me, but they weren't. I'd ride up on the rumbling three-wheeler and stop. Then, I'd turn off the engine and watch for them. I started parking far away so they knew they were safe. Then, I stopped closer to them each visit. They would pop their heads out of the hole and look at me. I imagine they were curious and watching me too.

Another summer, there was a hole with mice babies on the edge of the yard. When I told Grandma about them, I saw her make a face. She didn't want more mice. I imagine they were killed after we left. My grandparents wouldn't have told me. They protected me.

The best summer was when I was thirteen, and a dog showed up. I was zipping around the front of the house on the red Honda when a movement caught my eye. When she heard the Honda, she turned and ran away. I thought *she must belong to a neighbor.* I asked about her at dinner that night, "Grandpa, who has the multi-colored dog?" Grandpa said, "Mmmm? What did it look like?" I said, "It's medium-sized, and I think it has blue eyes."

"Where did you see it?"

"Out in front of the house on the road. It ran away when I stopped the three-wheeler to see it. It looks really skinny." Grandma said, "Mmmm, maybe we could put some of our table scraps out for it."

"That is a great idea!" I was so excited.

The dog was terrified and wouldn't come near me for weeks. Each time I tried to get close, she would run away and hide. Then, I had some pot roast leftovers I took from the fridge. "Come on, I won't hurt you," I said in my most comforting voice. Finally, after weeks of food and patience, she warmed up to

Chad and me. We played with her for the rest of our visit. She had white paws and a half-blue eye on one side. Grandpa thought she was a Blue Healer mix. I called her Boots. Chad wanted to call her Buckwheat. After we left, she bonded with Grandma, Grandpa, and Uncle Gary. Everyone loved Boots. She was a fantastic dog. In 1994, during my grandmother's funeral, Uncle Gary told this story:

"Boots disappeared the day my mother went into the hospital with heart issues. My mother had one good clear day before she passed away, and Boots was there on the farm wagging her tail for her final goodbye on that day, too. Boots disappeared, and Mom passed away on the same day."

Years later, when my mom was living on the farm, she removed the bushes from the front of the house. She found the bones from Boots with a stone shaped like a heart in the middle. I call this evidence. Evidence there is a power greater than me, and she shows herself in animals, nature, and miraculous things happening. I still have Boot's heart rock today.

Chapter Nine
Middle School

One of my seventh-grade teachers used their curriculum to show us *The Bill Wilson Story*. Bill Wilson was one of the founders and the primary author of the book Alcoholics Anonymous (The Big Book) and was responsible for creating the infrastructure of service. As I watched, I kept thinking about my dad. He spent a lot of time at the bar and drank beer every night. I had heard my mom call him an alcoholic. The definition in the movie was a person who couldn't stop drinking, even if they wanted to. In class, the teacher said, "An alcoholic was a person who would get drunk even when they didn't want to." *I wanted to get drunk; therefore, I would never become an alcoholic like my dad. I don't get drunk every day.* I thought. My inner child alcoholic was going to figure out a way to drink and not become a real alcoholic. Once I had this idea in place, my drinking no longer had any limits. I believed I was immune. I had found the right way to drink.

When I turned 16, my mom bought me a car, a small white 1974 Honda Civic hatchback, for my birthday. It was a stick shift, and it was like driving a go-cart. I was into drinking, smoking pot, music, and sex. Getting a set of wheels made it all sweeter. The combination was powerful and dangerous.

I had a birthday in April, but I was a year ahead of most other kids in my class because I had been held back in second grade. I was the only student in middle school with a driver's license and a car. A classmate I knew had a boyfriend named Ty. I didn't know him well, but she and I were in a few classes together, so I had heard her mention him several times. Ty was a 5'7" athlete with dark hair and light eyes. He arrived in my life at the same time as the car. He was exciting, dangerous, and fun. He was into sex, drugs, and having a good time. He could charm a room, and everyone always greeted him when he walked in the door. As soon as he found out I had a car, he became my new best friend. He was popular, and everyone knew who he was. The first time I felt noticed by Ty, I was standing at my locker, and I heard him say my name. "Hey, Janna." I turned around. "Oh, hey there Ty,"

"What are you doing tonight?"

"Um, I work until 7."

"Cool, want to pick me up at 7:30?" He asked. "Sure, okay." It was flattering to have his attention. He grabbed my hand as he walked away. When I tried to include his girlfriend in our meetups, he told me he had broken up with her. I wanted to believe him. He often arranged a time and place for me to pick him up while we were at school. I thought I was unique and important to him. I was desperate for his approval, affection, and attention, and he came with excitement and fun. *This guy is dangerous, and I could get hurt, but I can handle it.* I thought many times. My inner addict jumped into the deep end as fast as she could.

We went to college parties on campus, and I met many college-aged people who liked to drink the way I did. He knew where to find booze, drugs, and a good time, and I was his ride. I remember going out with him one night to play pool. We went to a pool hall on campus. It was a big room with windows in the front and two rows of pool tables lined up; behind the tables, there was a long wooden polyurethane-covered bar with backless stools. I didn't spend much time on campus and wasn't sure where we were in town. When I came out of the bathroom, I heard him saying, "Yeah, she can drink as much as I can and be just fine, man." Then, when he saw me, he grabbed me around my waist and pulled me in close to him with a big smile. He had a pint of rum, and we were drinking it fast. I don't remember leaving the pool hall, but I remember coming to and realizing I was driving my car with no consciousness. Chills ran up the back of my neck, and I felt sick to my stomach. My soul shuttered. I knew I could blackout again at any moment, and I was driving. When I told Ty I needed to pull over, he said, "No, you're doing great." I didn't want to seem like I couldn't keep up with him, so I kept driving.

The following day, I woke up in bed with my mind spinning. *What am I doing? That wasn't fun; I could've killed us last night. At least I was with Ty; he can handle anything.* It was my first dangerous blackout, but not my last.

Later that month, Ty took me to a friend's house, and we all hung out in the basement. We were drinking and smoking pot. I was trying to get numb, but the drugs and alcohol weren't working. I was still feeling anxious and uncomfortable in my skin. The next thing I remember was in a room with Ty. We were lying on someone's waterbed, and he was kissing me and removing my clothes. When we were done, he said, "wait here." He left, and another boy came in. This boy had been talking to me a lot that night, and I thought he was a sweet guy. "Oh, shit," I said as I pulled up the sheets to cover my naked body. "Hi," he said. "Ty told me to come in here."

"He did?" I said, shocked.

"Yeah, he told me you're cool." *Don't mess this up; they think you're cool.*

"Okay," He crawled into bed with me, and we started kissing. When we were done, he left. I just laid there. *What are you doing? Ty is going to be furious. This is bad. You are bad.* I dressed and went out into the living room. Ty was snuggled up on the couch with someone else. I felt hurt, stupid, and jealous. *Why'd I do that? Why is he with her now? What am I doing? What if I get pregnant? How will I know who the father is? I am a horrible person! I am so twisted.*

I had crossed an invisible line into the world of promiscuous, dangerous behavior. I thought my behavior would make things better for me. I thought I could numb my feelings. I felt ashamed, used, and unlovable, *but I'm cool. Right?* I wasn't afraid of dangerous situations because I had grown up with dangerous people all around me. I believed I could handle anything. Having people in my life who didn't care for me wasn't new either. I continued to party with this group of guys and ignored the pain and confusion I felt. I convinced myself it was all worth it because I was having a good time. I was not in touch with my feelings or my instincts. I knew how to keep secrets. I had expert training in the don't think, don't feel, don't talk, don't tell method of *Lives in Trauma*, and I survived the training.

A few months later, I was at a party with Ty and the gang; we were in a split-level house, standing by the front door in the living room. I had just smoked a bowl when my brother Chad walked in the front door. He was holding a cup, and his pupils were tiny and had a glossy sheen. I recognized the look from other people. He had a huge, easy grin on his face. "Hey, sis. What's up?" he says coolly. "Chad, what are you doing here?" I spit out. "Same as you, having a good time." He says pointedly. I was caught, ashamed, and speechless. *Yep, you're busted. He's doing the same messed up things you are, and he is cool. You're awkward, and no one really likes you.*

I left the party soon after I saw him. I thought I was responsible for him, but my time to party became more important than anything or anyone in my life. I had crossed the line to being a real alcoholic and didn't feel a thing.

Chapter Ten
Addiction

I went to a high school with an "open campus" policy. Our school was in an old brick colonial-style building with hardwood floors and lockers lining the hallways. The students were allowed to leave the school property for lunch. There were few places to eat nearby. There were a couple of college frat houses across the street and some small business buildings, but mostly, it was a residential neighborhood.

In the late 80s, all fast food was junk, high in saturated fats, and low in fiber and nutritional value. Close by the high school was a gas station and a Taco Bell. I would only go if other students asked me to join them; the rest of the time, I just didn't eat. There were no Smoothie King, Chipotle, or Mad Greens. I still ate the "long shelf-life" boxed foods and sugary snacks at home. I was still suffering from heartburn, constipation, and headaches. My emotional life, body image, and spiritual life were in turmoil. My emotions would change from moment to moment, and I wasn't mature or mentally resilient enough to manage them. I felt angry or sad in dramatic swings. I rarely had kind thoughts about myself. *I look like a pear, and I have huge hips with thick thighs. No wonder no one wants to stay with me. I am so awkward and dumb.*

I'd been dabbling in new-age thinking around God that involved tarot cards, the stars and planets, and crystals. However, I had no Higher Power. I thought God didn't care about me, or I would've been different, and I would've had parents who could care for me.

My sugar addiction really took hold with my job at a local ice cream parlor. There was a train track encompassing the ceiling, a to-go ice cream counter, and a restaurant in the back. I was a dishwasher and ice cream scoop. An old-fashioned round buttoned cash register made the ambiance festive, and everyone loved the train with its whistle and chug-a-chuga chuga-a-chuga moving around the perimeter. I loved ice cream. I ate a lot of free ice cream while working there. I started as a size six and left as a size fourteen seven months later. I remember the ice cream scoops sat in warm, water-filled metal scoop holders to cut through the hard ice cream. The smell of dairy, caramel, vanilla, and chocolate filled the air when the glass cover was lifted to serve up a scoop.

My older brother had moved back, and the verbal bullying was in full swing. "What's up, chocolate thighs?" Sean would greet me. I felt unsafe with him back at home. His verbal abuse seemed to validate the negative thinking already cutting at my weak self-esteem. He and my mom were fighting, too. She'd scream at him, and he'd yell back at her.

Fast food, ice cream, movie popcorn, and vast amounts of alcohol were the staples of my eating when I did eat. I was in an unhealthy cycle of eating nothing for many hours and then binging on sugary processed foods. I lost weight shortly after I stopped working at the ice cream parlor. However, I didn't lose the belief that I was fat. Socially, I felt awkward, unique, and alone. I was only comfortable socializing with alcohol and drugs influencing me.

I started hanging out with kids from another school, and I liked having one set of friends at my school and a separate group at a different school. I could party and get drunk and high, and I didn't have to live with everyone knowing about my behavior. The separation kept me hidden at both schools. At my school, I was the unpopular singing girl; at the other school, I was anonymous. The kids I was drinking and drugging with only talked about me with each other.

"Janna, who? No, I don't know her."

I could drink, drug, and have sex without the rumor mill talking about my behavior. There were no cell phones or social media to out me. Other schools were the competitors across town; the adults had made the physical lines, providing me with a way to act out anonymously. I lived for the parties with my "real" friends from the other school and couldn't wait to smoke pot and binge on peanut butter. I'd eat an entire jar with a spoon. It was the only time I felt I could let go of control and eat.

When I was seventeen, I started dating a guy from my mother's small hometown in Nebraska. He had blue eyes and long curly hair and played the drums. When he and I went to a local party with Chad, he introduced us to Reed. Reed knew all the local hangouts and where to find good parties. Reed was like a brother to me.

One chilly fall night, when my whole family was staying at Grandpa and Grandma's farmhouse. My dad was there visiting, too. Grandpa and Grandma were in Texas in their "winter house." The drummer and I had broken up. Reed pulled up in his white Ford 250 and slid his tires into the gravel. Chad and I were standing on the concrete steps by the dinner bell. Reed yelled out his window, "Hey there! Are you guys ready to hit the road?"

"Yeah, dude." My brother replied.

Reed, Chad, and I were drinking tequila. I drank to numb the ache in my chest. I was still heartbroken, and my head was spinning with thoughts of getting even. I felt resentful and filled with grief, and I didn't want to feel anything. I drank long, deep pulls from the bottle. The rest of the night was a blur. I remember falling out of the truck when Reed dropped us off at the farm. "Hey, I think you're so lucky. Life is easier for boys. I wish I was a boy." I slurred as Chad walked ahead and opened the squeaky metal screen door, "Shhhh," he said with his finger over his lips and an eye roll. "I'm goin' ta town," I said. "Whatever," Chad replied as he disappeared into the house.

I decided I'd walk to town and find the drummer. I was so drunk I blacked out and came to in the middle of the gravel road, about one mile from the farmhouse. I returned to awareness, laying on the gravel with goosebumps all over my cold skin. Boots, our farm dog, was licking my face. I struggled to stay aware and couldn't figure out where I was at first. I tried to pick up my head and look around. Then I saw the farm light. It was tiny and seemed very far away. I told Boots, "Please help me get back to the farm." There was nothing out there but plowed dirt fields and gravel roads. It was extremely dark. I didn't know it yet but I lost my scarf on the road where Boots was licking my face. Each time I started to black out, I would fall to my knees, and Boots would lick my face again. She helped me back to the farmhouse. Once I was in the house, I climbed three steps into the kitchen and made it to the doorway into the living room. I blacked out and fell to the ground again.

My older brother was sleeping on the couch in the living room and screamed at me to "shut up!" His abruptness brought me out of my blackout for a brief moment. I must have been crying and talking as I lay there. It was an ugly scene, and I was the star actress. When I look back at this night, there is no denying I am an alcoholic and powerless over alcohol. I would have done anything not to feel my feelings, including disrupting my family time and almost killing myself with too much tequila. I cannot imagine living like this, and yet I know I behaved this way again and again.

The morning came without my permission, and my knees and shins were covered in dried blood, scrapes, and cuts from crawling on the gravel, trying to get back to the farmhouse. I came to with my mother screaming, "Who threw up all over Grandma's wool carpet?"

"Janna, wake up! You threw up on Grandma's wool rug?"

I was trying to open my eyes, but my head was pounding, and when I opened my eyes, the brightness of the sun shut them again. The whole room was spinning. *What wool rug?* I thought. "It was not me. Settle down. I don't feel good, and you are hurting my head." I mumbled toward my mom. "I cannot believe you would act this way!" she said with disgust. "SSSHHHHH!" I rolled over and went back to sleep as the realization sank in that I did smell like vomit.

My alcoholic ego denied what I was responsible for, and I had no thoughts about anyone or anything except myself in that moment. I was in danger and needed help. There was none. My whole family, my mom, dad, and brothers, witnessed my alcoholism. When I finally roused, later than was normal for me, my family told stories of the night's events while I was blacked out. I had embarrassed myself. I didn't feel ashamed about anything except the harm to my grandma's carpet at that moment. I had watched both my parents act this way for my whole life. I didn't feel ashamed or guilty until my cousin's husband came in, carrying my scarf. My cousin's husband was a well-known, successful farmer in this small town. He found my scarf on the road.

He looked at me as he walked up the stairs from the porch. "Is this your scarf?"

"Er, um, yeah," I said. I couldn't look him in the eyes. I felt a punch in my stomach. "Thanks," I mumbled and looked down at the floor. "Janna, your scarf was in a low part of the road. If a car had come upon you... it would've run you over. You need to be more careful." He said with a knowing stare. *Shit, the whole town knows already.* Then, I felt the heat move from my stomach to my face. I couldn't stay in the kitchen and listen to them talk about all I had done. I walked outside, and Boots was there waiting for me, her tongue hanging out and her tail wagging. I gave her a hug and whispered, "Thank you," then we walked around the farm, and I prayed. *God, if you keep people from telling my grandparents, I swear I will never do this again.* I don't know if anyone ever told my grandparents.

This was the first time I thought *I might be an alcoholic.* I found a heart-shaped rock as I walked and prayed. I kept the rock to symbolize my commitment to staying sober. It didn't stick. I still had excuses left to tell. *I am too young, and I still go to school and work. I still have friends and family around me. I drink less than my parents. I just need to plan better. My life has been unfair, and I deserve to relax and take a break.* The alcohol was still working to numb my pain and fears, so I wasn't done yet.

"The world breaks everyone, and afterward, many are strong at the broken places."

– Ernest Hemmingway

Chapter Eleven
Broken

I had been dating a nice boy a few weeks before my graduation. He and I were in chorus class together. He drew and wrote poetry. He introduced me to the Beatles White album. We had gone to prom, and we were back at my trailer. My mom and Chad were gone.

"Hey, you want some champagne?" I asked as I stood in the cool air from the fridge. "No, I am good," he replied. I wanted to get drunk and sleep together after the dance. The familiar heat spread out in my body, and I turned away from him to hide my hurt. I had revealed my inner addict to a kind, good person, and I felt the shame.

On May 19, 1991, he broke up with me. *You're not good enough for a nice guy like that. You do not deserve him.* My inner critic shamed me.

On May 20, 1991, my cat, Niki, became violently ill. The doctor told me Niki had drank some antifreeze and been fatally poisoned. I stood in the operating room with Niki on the bright silver table. Her warm, fluffy body was not moving, but her eyes were open, and she looked into my eyes.

"I am sorry; I recommend that she be put to sleep to avoid any more suffering." I heard the veterinarian say.

Why am I here alone? I wish I had brought someone with me. I gave my consent and stayed with her as they injected the liquid into her veins. I heard her little scream as it went in; what a nightmare. My eyes burned and my heart was pounding in my ears. It was a horrible experience. *You did not protect her, and it is all your fault she suffered and died.* My pain body chided.

On May 22, 1991, Mom and I were up late. It was about 11:30 pm. My final singing performance was in a few days, and I asked Mom to help me make my costume. We had just completed, and we were cleaning up. The phone rang. I picked it up. "Hello."

"This is the police. Are you the parent of Chad"?

"No, hold on."

"Mom, it's the police." My mom gives me an 'oh shit' look. "Hello?"

"Yes...Oh my god, we will be right there." My mom's face is pale in an instant. "Janna, get dressed. We have to go to the hospital."

My younger brother had been in a car accident, and we needed to go to the hospital in a neighboring town right away. That was all we knew. When we arrived at the hospital, the woman at the front desk of the ER escorted us into a private room and closed the door. The room was a small rectangle with a bench seat on one wall and a couple of chairs on the other wall. There were no windows. It was painted a light mint green color. I sat on the bench, and my mom sat on a chair. We waited silently for what felt like a very long time—finally, a knock on the door. My mom opened the door. A man in light blue-green scrubs came in and sat down with a file in his hands. He closed the door and opened the manilla folder he carried with him. My body was shivering, and the room kept wobbling. "Are you Ann, Chad's mom?"

"Yes."

"Who is this?" He points at me. "This is his sister." He looks back at my mom. "Your son has been in a head-on collision; he has bruises all over his body, and his lower lip was split open. He needed a lot of stitches. He had 26 stitches on the inside of his lip and 48 stitches on the outside."

"Oh my God!" My mother's eyes widen, then stare at the blank wall. "Was there anyone else in the car?" She says without moving her eyes. "There was a girl and a boy." He says, "The girl has a shattered pelvis and will need extensive surgery."

"How's the boy?" My mom asks. The man looks at me. He takes a breath and says, "He didn't make it."

"Oh, God." My mom says, then drops her head onto her hands and starts to rock back and forth. I started shivering and felt cold on the inside of my skin. *He's gone. The funny, kind, charismatic, clever boy is gone. Chad's best friend is gone. He was only fifteen years old.* I was swimming through time. It felt unreal. I was in a dream. *This cannot be real.* Shock and denial overtook my brain. Another hospital person came and took my mom and me back to see Chad. His mouth was all jagged and swollen. The rims of his eyes matched his red, puffy lower lip. My mom hugged him and asked if he was alright. He was silent. The police came into the room, and they put handcuffs around his wrists. I watched the police take my younger brother to jail.

My mom contacted her cousin, who lived in the same town. "Sue, I need a place to go and wait until I can see Chad in Jail." She lived nearby, and we stayed at her house until we could visit Chad.

My mom was standing in the kitchen with the refrigerator door open. She looked up at the ceiling, closed the door, and said, "Oh my God! I can never drink again." I was sitting at the kitchen table, and I thought *my mom is falling apart. Okay, okay, okay, I can handle this.* I watched her pace around the kitchen, and she talked about her decision never to drink again. I couldn't understand why she said, "I can never drink again." Repeatedly. *She is in shock. I just need to be ready for her to fall apart.*

A few hours later, we arrived at a cinder block building on the outskirts of town. It was sunny and windy outside. There was no landscaping and a flagpole with a flag blowing in the wind. The parking lot was mostly empty, with only a few cop cars parked on the side. When we walked in, there was a reception area with windows from the countertop up to the ceiling. We had to give them our purses and sign a sheet of paper on a clipboard. A police officer escorted us down a hallway. Then she unlocked the door into a room. It was a small room with Pepto-Bismol-colored walls. Chad was sitting on the metal bed; his body was slumped over. When he looked up, I could see his red-rimmed blue eyes. Chad told us what he knew about his upcoming court date.

The next day, I drove to school for my afternoon singing class. I arrived just before the fifth period and had to park on the opposite side of the school from where the music department was. I walked to the heavy metal double door and walked up the stairs to the second floor in numb silence. Then, I opened a second door to the long hallway. I started down the hall, and as I walked, I noticed a bubble of silence surrounding me. I could hear loud voices ahead of me and loud whispers behind me, but it was completely silent as I passed. I heard a girl behind me saying, "That's her!" As I walked, my cheeks started to burn, and my legs felt weak. My stomach clenched, and my heart pounded. Shame laid over me like a heavy shawl. *Is this really happening? How did everyone know? I didn't tell anyone. I know how to keep things like this to myself. I am anonymous.* I went to my locker, and Margret was there. I saw deep emotion on her face, and she hugged me and said, "I am so sorry." My skin felt too tight. My head was hot. *How does she know?* I looked around, and people were still looking at me. The hall where I was had a heavy, thick silence lingering behind me. I grabbed my sheet music and walked quickly toward the back of the school where my class was. I walked up the three levels of risers to the chair I sat in with the other sopranos. "Are you okay?" My friend Joanna asked. I looked at her and said, "How does everyone know what happened?"

"The school administration announced Chad's drunk driving accident and said a student was killed." The heat exploded throughout my whole body, and I felt sweat under my arms. My ears began to ring. I felt hot with anger, hurt, betrayal, and shame. I wanted to be anonymous. *They told my story, my brother's story. They said his name. Why would they do that? Why did they tell the whole school what happened? I don't belong here. People hate me. I am an outsider. I am different. I am poor and live in a trailer. They all have money and two parents.*

No adults showed up for me again. I was invisible to the adults while under a magnifying glass from people my age. When other students entered the room, they quieted as soon as they saw me. It felt like something was pushing down on my head. It was quiet until the teacher began to teach. *This is stupid. I need to leave.* I stood up and jumped down from the top level halfway through class. My teacher didn't try to stop me. I ran down the hallway and out to my car as fast as my legs would allow. Then I drove away from the school.

I don't remember the amount of time between when Chad went to jail and court. I had never been to a courtroom before, and I decided to wear a dress; my body felt like it weighed a ton. I couldn't get warm, so I sat on the hard wooden bench and shivered. The large room had many long rows of wooden benches that reminded me of the benches in my grandparent's Lutheran church. I saw a stage with chairs off to the left side of the judge. *It looks like a church.* I thought. *Interesting that both a courtroom and a church are places of judgment and are designed with hard wooden benches. Please God help us.* My mom sat in the courtroom beside Chad; I sat alone behind them. The judge walked in, and he sat down in his chair. He looked down at Chad. Then his eyes moved to my mom and finally landed on me. *I am glad I wore a dress today.* I heard the judge say the name of the deceased boy's mom. She stood up, and the judge asked her what she'd like to say: "I ask that Chad get help; treatment will be better than jail." She said in a shaky voice.

This brave, beautiful mother showed compassion, kindness, and grace toward my brother. At that moment, the trajectory of my life changed. She must have understood addiction and family illness or had support from a wise person. I think of her with gratitude and send up prayers that she and the boys' sister have peace and joy. I think about them often.

Chad was made a ward of the state and placed in a treatment center for youths. My mom, Chad, and I went to the 15-year-old boy's funeral. After the service, I was outside near the back doors and getting ready to return to the funeral home, and I felt a hand on my arm. I looked up, and there was a dark-haired older woman. She said in a clear, strong-soft voice, "It's all going to be okay." I believed her. I felt peace and warmth come over me. I looked down, and she was gone when I looked back up. *Did I just meet an angel?* I wondered.

A few weeks after the accident, I graduated from high school, and my dad and maternal grandparents were all in town for my concert, graduation, and party. My mom had a friend who lived in a condominium association with a clubhouse. It was a nice part of town and a great place for a gathering. Chad had a pass from treatment to attend my celebration. It no longer felt like a graduation party for me. Chad's friends were there, my mom's friends were there, and a few people showed up for me. I'm grateful to them for being there. I still felt protective of Chad at the time, and it seemed okay for it to be about him.

When my mom read the speech she had prepared, her voice cracked when she talked about my being a good sister to Chad. My mom tried to celebrate my graduation, but she wasn't able to get out of her own way. In all fairness, I was focused on him too.

Chapter Twelve
Higher Power Tree

July 4, 1991. I was doing what I always did for the 4th of July. I went to City Park, where people ate, drank, talked, played games, and saved their area for the fireworks show later in the night sky. City Park was huge, and there were always lots of people spread out on the grass with their coolers, blankets, chairs, and games. I was there with my newly sober mom and brother. I walked around and saw people I knew, and everyone wanted to know how Chad was doing. I saw a guy I had admired from afar for years, and when he approached me, it seemed like we connected. "Hi Janna, how are you?"

"I am good. How are you?" I replied. "I am good." We talked for a bit, and then he invited me to join him at a party in mid-July. I was so flattered and excited he wanted to spend time with me. We set a date for the party, then sat and watched the fireworks together. The 4th of July guy and I went out on our first date. It was going well until we arrived at the party. We walked up to the house, and I could hear the music and see there were a lot of people inside. My stomach started to do flips as we walked in the door. I didn't know anyone, and my heart sped up. My hands felt sweaty, and there was a lump in my throat. A huge punch bowl full of Tom Collins was sitting on the counter in the kitchen. He handed me a red Solo cup and filled it with punch. It was the first situation I had been in after my brother's accident where there was alcohol. I looked at the drink and felt a catch in my breath. My stomach clenched. My brain started to spin. I hadn't had a drink since the accident. *Should you drink?* My new healthy voice asked. *Why not?* My inner addict answered. I took a huge gulp of air. *Breathe.* I started to feel more at ease inside my head. *See!* My inner addict boasted: *let's get drunk. It'll feel good.*

I looked around at all the strange faces and felt uncomfortable. I tallied up the alcohol compared to the number of people. I realized there wasn't enough alcohol to get totally numb. I looked at the guy I was with, and he gave me his kind, gentle smile. *He is such a nice guy. You do not deserve this guy. You're going to mess it up. If you continue to drink, you'll ruin the night for him too.* This new healthy voice was no longer in denial about how bad it would get. *Remember the boy.* The new voice reminded me.

I knew I could die, or someone could die if I continued to drink. I had no idea how not to drink. For the second time in my life, I think *you're an alcoholic; you're obsessed with getting a drink now. There is help.* I shut down and withdrew from everyone at the party. I sat on the side of a couch on the floor where no one could see me. I tried to be invisible. "Hey, Janna, are you okay?" My date asked. "No. Can you take me home, please?" He did, and I never saw him again.

Chad's best friend died in that car accident, and I knew for me that to drink is to die. Some people die slowly, like my dad, and some die quickly, like the fifteen-year-old boy. I committed to treating my life differently to honor my brother, my mom, and that boy. I planned on taking steps toward healthy living and making a change for the better. I started the long journey from Sunshine to Soulshine.

I found other sober people who shared my new resolve and my journey. We started spending time together. We talked about new habits to support this different way of life. I felt heard, seen, and believed by my new friends. They were honest and talked about their feelings. They talked about how to heal and recommended helpful approaches. I found a spiritual mentor, and she guided me in finding a Higher Power to support my decision to be clean and sober. She told me I was beyond human aid and cautioned me against having a Higher Power that mimicked human traits. The confusing, incongruent messages I received as a child about love and the disappointment I felt from authority figures made this accurate for me. My Higher Power had to be non-human, and I worked at finding a connection with nature as my physical symbol of my Higher Power.

One day, while driving down the main street of my hometown, I saw a perfect tree covered in frost and snow. *That's it!* My healthy voice sang. *I found my Higher Power!* It was beautiful and majestic, and I felt warm, light energy in my body. I could see this Higher Power. In my mind, I could hear the wind in the leaves, and I could touch the bark. There was energy radiating from the tree. My soul hummed.

I didn't have the words to name the feelings, but I knew it was good. I decided that a snow-frosted tree would be my Higher Power. The symbol of it, anyway. Thankfully, I continued to grow in the concept of what my Higher Power was to me. As I became healthy, I found the source of my Higher Power in all of nature, and when I was out on a hike or a walk, I gained peace and energy from all the earth surrounding me. I believed my deep connection to nature led me to future decisions to protect her, but more about that later.

At the beginning of my sober life, habits became needed tools for the resilience I had to build for my continued sobriety. I made my bed in the morning, then prayed. It helped me remember if I had prayed or not each day. When I removed the decorative pillows at night, it reminded me to look at my day and review it with a critical eye for possible harm I had caused. I started to think of kinder, more loving, healthier thoughts; *who do I know that is struggling with drinking? Have I hurt anyone? Do I owe any amends, or do I need to clean up old wounds within myself and with others?* Then, I prayed for people suffering and people I loved. This habit supported the new voice in my thoughts. *What if I focus on one thing every year? I could become my best self.*

I'd seen the possibility of real growth and improvement in my life. I was motivated by past suffering to make the changes I needed to find the life I wanted. I decided each year, on my sobriety anniversary in July, I would select a focus. Something I could really practice.

The shame voice argued: *You are broken, and you'll need to be perfect to be loveable. You can't stay sober.*

I heard people in my sober circle discussing new ideas, like balance, self-care, serenity, and willingness. *These ideas will improve my life.* Those were the topics I would choose as my beginning focus. In the following years, these focuses came together to create health and healing in my life. I now share these years of healing with all of you.

Chapter Thirteen
Balance

When I chose balance, I was using the definition of a state in which things occur in equal or proper amounts. The goal was to create equal and proper amounts of work, college, and recovery. These three things were all important to me. I settled on three items because the number three resonated with me. It was a good start in shaping my new healthy life.

I moved to Denver for a Sign Language Interpreter Training program. I would graduate with an Associate of Applied Science degree in two years and become an American Sign Language Interpreter.

When I was in college, I started to have more acne, I was still struggling to eliminate waste daily, and I had frequent headaches. I was dating, and many of these things compounded how I criticized myself and my body. I felt awkward and embarrassed while I was around other people. I'd been living sober for a couple of years, and I had begun therapy. My therapist told me I was anorexic. She signed me up for group therapy. I would meet with other people who also had eating disorders. I struggled to relate with the overeaters. I would think *I'm different; I don't ever overeat, and I am in control of myself.* I didn't realize that control would be the mountain I would one day have to climb to find peace and love in my life. I was not different from others.

I thought I needed balance, with the real goal of more control. I learned about setting boundaries in group therapy. The motive behind most of my boundaries was rooted in controlling the people and the environment around me. Control did help me feel safe, but it fed the critical monster and sabotaged my life. The sober community was abuzz about boundaries too.

I was hired at several restaurants during the years I was in college. I worked at an Italian bistro restaurant for a year and began to look at food differently. I watched the chef and sous chef as they chopped, sliced, and diced food. My mind started to open to new foods and new ways of combining them. I learned to describe menu items like arugula, asparagus, artichokes, balsamic vinaigrette, fresh cracked pepper, basil, oregano, and thyme. I was learning which foods paired together well. They added a sushi option, but I was too afraid to try it. I was curious and watched him make it, and I asked many questions. I believed meat must be cooked at high temperatures, or I would get sick. It challenged my beliefs about meat. There was also a balance in the portion of fish compared to the grain and vegetables in a sushi roll, which I was curious about.

I spent this year looking at balance, so I divided my time between work, college, and sobriety into thirds. I tried to create some play time and quickly learned that playing for me was about learning; as long as I was learning new things, I was playing. I would call my new spiritual mentor to explain/complain, and she would listen patiently. When I was all done, she would simply say, "It's time to get busy, Janna." I interpreted her message to mean it does me no good to just talk about issues; I needed to learn to take action to change them if I could. I started to understand that if all I did was talk about an issue and didn't take action, I was just complaining. She taught me the Serenity Prayer:

God grant me the serenity to accept the things I cannot change, courage to change the things I can, and the wisdom to know the difference.

Courage to change the things I can. I have come to know the only things I can change are my feelings, behaviors, and beliefs. *The wisdom to know the difference* is knowing what I can do to change myself, not others. Balance was when my inner life and my outer life matched or when they became congruent. My thinking, feeling, and acting would all align with my values. Learning to balance my life would take a lifetime, but I grew closer to finding my balance each year.

Chapter Fourteen
Get Busy

"Get busy" was such a helpful phrase because I learned how to deal with uncomfortable things. I began the practice of doing what I didn't want to do and I kept going until it was done.

Growing up, there were no adults around to guide me in building structure for undesirable tasks such as doing my homework. Instead, I sat in front of the TV and binge-watched television and, ate sugary cereal or mac and cheese and drank wine. When my critical, negative voice started to complain, *you're poor; you're not getting enough attention, you're not* - fill in the blank. I would think, *can I change this?* If the answer was *yes.* Then, it was time to *get busy.*

My first spiritual mentor helped me to look at my behaviors and how those behaviors caused me anxiety. My second spiritual mentor was helping me see the patterns in my behavior. One of the biggest patterns we identified was when I thought a person didn't like me, I would focus on trying to manipulate or control them with kindness and generosity to get them to like me. Then, when they behaved the same way as they always had, I would get angry and cut them off and judge them. It was a game that wasted my time and energy. I was contributing to my false self when I played this game.

The Serenity Prayer talked about acceptance. I knew I needed to accept I couldn't control how other people felt about me. I became more aware I needed to accept my thoughts and be more curious about other people. My spiritual mentors spent hours answering my questions. I always had questions. They were patient and provided me with thorough responses.

My mentor explained, "When you ask questions, you have a responsibility to remain open-minded." I liked anything that required me to take responsibility, and being open-minded became my goal for the next year.

Chapter Fifteen
Open Minded

Open-minded is defined in Webster's Dictionary as receptive to arguments or ideas. Receptive was an idea that would immediately be helpful. Receptive wasn't about control; it was receiving instead of giving. Control was given from me to others. To be in acceptance and open was a practice in receiving. It was a good beginning practice.

On a cold day in December, I arrived at college and my professor, Linda said, "Janna can you come into my office? Bring a friend, too." My close friend was standing next to me, so I looked at her. "Will you come with me?" I asked. She gave me a comforting smile and replied, "Yes!"

We walked down the hall to the professor's office. I walked in first and sat in the old wooden chair against the wall next to her desk. I felt wiggly, and my heart was speeding up. I could normally read people well and guess what was coming. I had no idea what she would say. I imagined the worst. *You really messed up, and she is going to kick you out of the program. I'm sure you deserve whatever is going to happen to you.* "Am I in trouble?" I asked as my foot moved back and forth quickly. Linda replied, "Oh gosh no." Then she looked at my friend and back at me with a nervous glance. Then she looked down at her desk.

"Um, Janna. Your mom called here this morning. Your grandmother passed away." I didn't have a landline or a cell phone at the time, so my mom called the only place she knew she could find me. How unfortunate for my professor to have to tell me this horrible news. My face fell, and I looked at the floor, my eyes filled with big, hot tears. I felt a tightness in my heart. My world became instantly darker. *Grandma is gone. I did not get to call her and tell her I love her. I suck. I have finals, and I will not abandon what I am responsible for. I will stay and complete my finals.* The grief had not fully consumed me yet.

Linda spoke up, "You don't need to stay for the finals; you can leave. There is a phone and a private office in room 203B that you can use for as long as you want. Here is the number for your mom if you need it."

"Thanks," I said. I was in shock. I went to the room alone and called my mom. We came up with a plan. I would have time to take my finals. After my last one, I would drive an hour to my hometown and pick up my mom. Together, we would drive to the farm late that evening.

At that time, my family believed in open-casket viewing. I was very young when my great-grandpa Harvey passed, and I saw him lying there dead. I had nightmares for months. It was creepy and disturbing to me. "Mom, will Grandma Alice be in a coffin for the world to see?"

"Yes, that is what we do. It helps people accept and process that a person is really gone."

"I don't need to see them all dead to accept that they are really gone, and it creeps me out."

"Oh?" pause. "Well," pause. "I guess I never thought about having it any other way."

"Okay, well, when I die, if I go first, no coffin." I declared.

71

"Okay," Pause. "I think I want to be cremated; it seems like a waste of good earth to bury people." My mom replied.

We talked openly and honestly for the next three hours. It was a slow, calm pace; I felt heard by my mom for the first time in my life. Sobriety was changing our relationship, and I believed there was hope for us to heal. I lost my grandmother, who loved me fiercely, and I started to build a new friendship with my sober mom. I worked hard to stay open-minded about our future.

In my sobriety, I wanted to become a happy whole person. I wanted a joyful life. I thought I could make myself perfect. April 19, 1995, I was in my studio apartment getting ready for my college classes; I was listening to the news, "In Oklahoma City just a moment ago at the Alfred P. Murrah Federal Building, a car bomb exploded." *What did they say?* I walked out of the bathroom and stood in front of my TV.

"It seems a white supremacist group is taking credit for the bombing. They selected this day as it was Hitler's birthday. Other events that have occurred on this day include 1775, the battle of Lexington began, and the shot was heard around the world. (The day before was when Paul Revere took his famous ride.) In 1882, Charles Darwin died. In 1889, Adolf Hitler was born. In 1993, eighty members of the millennial Branch Davidian religious group perished in their compound in Waco, Texas."

My heart started to pound. *This is Hitler's birthday too? No wonder I'm such a horrible person and cannot have healthy relationships with other people. My friend Quinn committed suicide one year ago today. This day is cursed. My birthday is cursed.* These details fueled the already burning fire of shame, self-judgment, and harshness toward myself. While I no longer feel shame and self-judgment, I still pray nothing horrible happens every year on my birthday. I also remember all those who have suffered and died from all the events and the ripples of those events in our Universe.

My cousin moved to Denver, and we rented an apartment together. It was closer to my college and would cut down on the traveling through the city. She was a good cook and would take a boxed meal and add more ingredients. Sometimes, she'd add more noodles or frozen or canned vegetables to make it a better meal. I learned a lot from watching her cook while we lived together.

When I moved out to my own apartment, I felt like maybe I'd try to cook for myself. A friend from college was on Atkins and told me to give it a try. I was struggling with gas, acne, and headaches, and I was willing to try anything. I was learning about food prep at my job, so I thought doing some cooking without a box might be fun.

Atkins is a low carbohydrate diet, eliminating foods such as sugar, bread, pasta, milk, fruits, and some vegetables. A person can eat as many "high protein" foods like meat, cheese, and eggs. The idea is the body will burn fat instead of sugar. The diet encourages animal meat as the main source of protein. It was designed by Robert Atkins in the 1970s. It wasn't healthy for me, but it was a step toward learning a new way to interact with food and noticing how it affected me.

The best thing I learned about myself during this experiment was about gluten. Gluten is made up of two proteins, gliadin and glutenin, found in wheat, barley, and rye. It's used for its elasticity in making baked goods. When I stopped eating bread, my digestion changed. I was less constipated, had a lot less gas, and I had almost no headaches. I felt more energetic, too. When I'd try to add in bread again, I would get gassy, bloated, and achy. I would get a headache first. Then, the bloat and the gas.

Finally, I would have diarrhea about 24 hours later. It didn't take me long to realize I had to be allergic to gluten.

While following the Atkins diet, I learned to eat raw carrots and snack on raw almonds. These new learned habits benefited my diet in a healthier direction. I learned that in my body, gluten caused intestinal distress, headaches, and a general foggy mind. Atkins had a cookbook with some recipes that seemed simple. I bought it and would bring it to the grocery store with me. Change took time and money, but I began to buy peppers, cauliflower, mixed greens, almonds, cheese sticks, gluten-free flour, and meat. None of these ingredients were from a box. Raw veggies with ranch and some almonds became a meal. This was the first time I realized eating raw veggies was healthy and easy. No stove was needed—*what a relief.* I read and reread the directions, so I didn't make a mistake. I worked slowly and carefully. There were some directions I didn't understand so I tried to do the best I could.

The dollar store sold cheap kitchen supplies. I bought a measuring cup, a big bowl, and some measuring spoons. I had to look up terms I didn't know. Dicing, slicing, and chopping were different from each other, but I was unsure how. A low boil was a concept that blew my mind. Simmering was something I didn't understand in the kitchen. (or my emotional life.) Turning down the heat seemed like a waste of time. However, I learned by cleaning badly burned food off pans; I didn't like to waste time and food. After I ruined a couple of cheap pots, I began to turn down the heat. My plastic measuring cup was for wet ingredients like oil, vinegar, and water. I didn't realize there was a different kind of cup for dry ingredients such as flour, rice, and sugar. Until a little later. No wonder some of my meals were just a little too dry.

My downfall was my habit of eating fast food. I was eating at my restaurant more and learning how new vegetables tasted, but my habit still had me going to Wendie's and McDonald's too often.

In May of 1995, I graduated from college. After I graduated, I planned a trip to San Diego. My friends and I ate out at restaurants and traveled to a beach for some fun in the sun. While there, my friends and I decided to go to a fancy restaurant to eat fresh seafood. I grew up in a landlocked state and had never eaten fresh fish from the ocean prior to this trip. I knew it would be a good opportunity to be open-minded and try something new. I ordered tuna steak with a baked potato. The tuna was like butter in my mouth. I loved every bite of it. Food is memorable when it is fresh, cooked perfectly, and tastes delicious. The takeaway for me here was fresh. There is nothing fresh about long shelf life and boxed food. Food can bring freshness, energy, and joy, or it can bring disease, exhaustion, and sadness.

I have such great memories of that trip to San Diego. When I arrived home from San Diego, a former college classmate told me there was an interpreter job in Pennsylvania. She assured me I could have the job. I wanted to experience other areas of the country and I thought *this is my chance*. My lease was over at the end of June. I packed up my little Honda Civic and moved to Pennsylvania.

Chapter Sixteen
Patience

I moved out East. Then, I landed a job with a school district in North Central Pennsylvania. The former classmate was not able to give me the job, but she helped me get an interview. After a second interview, I met the parents, who gave their approval. Then, I was offered the position. I had been patient, and it paid off.

I looked for opportunities to be patient. When I noticed a line was long, I chose to wait in the long line. Then at times, I would get pleasantly surprised, and it would end up moving faster than the short line. I focused my patience on others and things outside of myself. I didn't learn to be patient with myself right away. I still had expectations of perfection toward myself. I realized my expectations about how events should happen were a self-defeating habit. I learned it's about time. When I thought my time was being wasted or abused in some way, I wasn't patient. I started to ask myself. *What's the rush? Enjoy this experience, and maybe you'll learn something.*

I felt alone and lonely in Pennsylvania. Life out East was faster-paced than in the Midwest. I soon made some friends and started to adjust. I was beginning to hang out with a small group. We would go out to eat, go bowling, and play cards. One evening, I was invited to go bowling; I arrived late and saw a woman sitting at a counter on the outer perimeter. I took the seat next to her. She said, "Hi, I'm Mary. Do you know everyone?"

"No," I replied, feeling a little uncomfortable.

"Let me introduce you." One member of the crew was a man everyone called Tommy. "Tommy, come meet Janna. She's from Colorado." *This guy looks like Kenny Chesney. I would like to see him in a cowboy hat.* I thought. He was handsome, with dark shoulder-length hair and beautiful blue eyes. He hopped over to me, "Hi, I'm Tommy." He shook my hand and smiled.

"Hi, Tommy, my name's Janna."

"Hi, Janna!" then with a gust of wind, he was back on the wooden alley floor, pitching his hot pink ball at the pins.

"Strike!" he yelled with a jump and a fist pump. He was good at bowling.

He turned and smiled at me.

Later, I was told Tom was a clean and sober man from New Jersey. He was a charming Dead Head, and he played hockey. He had a bright smile, a clever sense of humor, and he was ready to try anything. We kept going out as a group and doing fun things together for several months. One of the crew kindly always made sure I was included.

One evening in January 1996, we were at Perkins, and Tommy had a newspaper in his hands. He said, "Oh cool, Natalie Cole is playing at the theater here." I said, "Oh, I like big band music!" I did like big band music, and I owned the *For The Boys* album from Bette Midler which I loved to play and sing to. I still do. A few weeks later, Tommy asked me to go to the concert with him.

We had our first date on February 13, 1996. On July 4, 1996, Tom and I were in New York City. Tom had been acting jumpy and anxious all day. He had pulled me around New York City, and I was getting irritated. I remember we were going to Macy's on the subway, and I said to him, "What is wrong with you today? Do we need to leave the city?" I was worried he wanted to use because we were in New York City. He had lived there while in his addiction.

We arrived at Macy's, and we looked around, but I didn't feel like shopping. As we were leaving, he started to act weird again. He was fiddling in his jacket and kept pointing to random buildings and saying, look at that one. I'd look in that direction and then think, "Which one?" He got on one knee as I turned around, but he couldn't get the box out of his jacket. I realized what was happening, so I turned away and started talking about the buildings. Finally, he said my name.

"Janna," he said with a soft intimacy. I turned around, and he was on one knee, holding open a ring box with a brilliant round solitaire diamond ring inside.

I said, "Yes!"

We hurried to the hotel in the World Trade Center Towers where we were staying. We checked in and spent time alone talking about our future together. Then, we called our families and shared the news with them. That night from the top floor of Tower II, we watched the fireworks all over the city. These memories are precious for me on many different levels today. I had prayed for patience, and I was about to put what I learned to good use.

Chapter Seventeen
Serenity

I planned the next three years words from the Serenity prayer. Serenity, Courage, and Wisdom.

I had done some reading about boundaries, and I thought they were the answer to a serene life. I believed if I set boundaries I would start to heal, and I knew healing would bring serenity. I was fearful that Tom would leave me if I wasn't perfect, but I was constantly in conflict between my fear of abandonment, and the lack of trust. *If he breaks it off, I will be alone forever. I don't think we are a good fit for each other. I hate his smoking. I am terrified he will leave me. Do I know what love is?* I thought if I set the right boundaries, my problems would be solved, and then I could feel serene. After we became engaged, I told him I wouldn't marry him if he didn't stop smoking. He would stop for a few days or weeks, then I'd smell it on him again. "Tom! Have you been smoking?" The control addict accused. "No!"

"Why do I smell smoke? I don't smell like smoke." He replied.

"Yes, you do!"

"Maybe it was _____" (any coworker or friend he could blame) "Oh. If you're smoking again, it's over! I told you, my boundary." *He's lying. Is he looking me in the eyes; maybe he is not lying. I'm so confused. I cannot leave him. I'm powerless over other people, so I can't control him. Can I trust him?*

This cycle of conflicting thoughts went on for years. I felt perpetually stuck in this situation and conversation. Each time I smelled smoke, the unsolved conflict set up camp in my mind. I was resentful about my parents' smoking and how I believed it affected my health. Now, I was engaged to a man that I thought was lying. Trust was fragile. I had very little for myself, and so there was very little for anyone else.

In August of 1996, we decided to move in together. I believed if we lived together, his smoking would stop. One night my anger had mounted to the point that I left his apartment. He chased me down the driveway and begged me to come back. I thought he would change. My control addict thought she could handle this confusing relationship. *He loves me, and we can get through anything that comes up.* I falsely convinced myself. We had planned our marriage for the Fall of the following year. I knew I needed time to get to know him better before I would be ready to marry him.

However, in September, I found out I was pregnant. I was determined to never be a single mother; I knew I had to do everything in my power to keep our relationship together. The control monster celebrated.

I remember during my grandparent's 75th wedding anniversary, a relative asked my grandparents, "What's your secret?" My Grandpa Carl had replied, "I followed my father's advice. My father told me to be committed to the marriage, not the person." I'd be committed to the marriage. I had a plan.

Tom and I were married on December 31, 1996. I wanted to look amazing on my wedding day, so my focus on food and eating kicked into high gear. I tried to eat healthily, but I only knew about Atkins. I eliminated bread and pasta, but I felt like I was missing out when I didn't eat bread. I must confess; I never did Atkins exactly how it was intended. I never stopped eating any of the veggies they suggested to eliminate. I knew in my soul carrots couldn't be bad. My grandma Alice had talked about veggies like they were necessary, and I believed her.

I've never been officially tested for Celiac Disease. To be tested, it was necessary to eat gluten again, and I wasn't interested in the consequences of eating gluten. I also didn't have any health insurance and didn't go to doctors. For years, when I met anyone who shared with me they had Celiac Disease, I would ask them many questions. Generally, people don't like to talk about digestive functions, but I've interviewed many people and am confident I am allergic to gluten. I also know I had my first pregnancy while abstaining from gluten at the age of 25. This is another piece of evidence of possible Celiac Disease.

I started to believe I could become a good cook if I were willing to open my mind and follow directions in a recipe. I bought the Betty Crooker cookbook. I had seen copies of this book on the shelves of my grandmother's and my mother's house. This book had a section where it defined the words for me. I was proudly up to two cookbooks and a small number of recipes I felt comfortable making. I learned to make gluten-free waffles, oatmeal, and stir fry. I also learned to eat mixed strawberries, apples, and blueberries or an apple with peanut butter. I was on my way.

I had an earned reputation for burning things. I remember years of preparing food and having a hard time with the "cooking" part. I didn't enjoy cooking, partly because it required patience to stand at the stove and wait for the food to heat up. I had very little patience for things I wasn't very skilled at doing. I falsely believed food would cook better and faster if I used high heat. I didn't realize it would also damage valuable nutrients and pots. I destroyed some quality pots as a teenager. It's a miracle I never burned down a house. My brothers would joke I knew the food was done because the fire alarm was going off. "Oh, Tom, I burned it again."

"It's not that bad; it tastes good to me. I am glad that you cooked, and I didn't have to. Thanks."

I'd burn big pots of food, and then I would separate the top layer of cooked food from the burned bottom layer, and we would eat what I salvaged. I'm very grateful he didn't criticize me. He held space for me to work through my anxiety and self-judgment. I didn't give up. I kept on trying with his support and encouragement. I became an expert at cleaning pots after I burned the food. I learned if I added water and soap to the burned pot and added heat the burned food would break down and scrape off more easily. My skills became résumé worthy. To his credit, my new husband didn't ever complain about my horrible food. *That was love.* The real rub was he was an excellent cook. His onion soup was legendary.

I was always good at macaroni and cheese because I could cook the noodles on high until they were soft and throw the hot noodles in a strainer. Then, turn off the heat and mix the butter, milk, and powdered cheese in the hot pot. Finally, I'd put the warm rinsed noodles on top of the mixture. The warm noodles would melt the butter, warm the milk, and melt the cheese. I mixed it all up, and it wasn't too hot to eat. It fit with my all-or-nothing thinking in the kitchen. I've eaten a lot of macaroni and cheese in my life. It is still comforting food for me. My children think I make the best mac and cheese in the world. That's something I am proud of.

Tom came home from work one day and saw what I was doing. "What are you making," he asked. "I found a gluten-free recipe for waffles, and you had a waffle iron so I thought I would try breakfast for dinner."

"Great! Can I help?"

"Um, if you really want to, but you don't need to."

"Can I see the recipe?"

"It's over on the table," I said.

"This is cool, Janna; it looks like this recipe uses a mixture of vinegar and baking soda to give rise to the waffles."

"What?"

"Yeah, it says to mix all the wet ingredients in a bowl and the dry ingredients in a bowl. Then, when the vinegar and baking soda get mixed, the batter fluffs up, like the volcanoes in school," he explained. "Oh, that is clever. I am curious about the apple cider vinegar in waffles; it sounds terrible."

"It's just a tablespoon. Shall I mix the dry stuff and you can mix the wet stuff?"

"Sure. I am almost done, then I'll give the measuring cup to you."

"Wet ingredients use different cups than dry ingredients." He explained.

"Oh?" I said. "Yeah, look." He filled the wet measuring cup with one cup of water, then he poured it into the dry measuring cup. "See, they are close but not the same." There was a bit of water left in the wet measuring container. Again, I was grateful for his support. It took me a long time to cook the most basic, simple recipes. I hung in there and worked hard at figuring it out though.

When I wasn't eating gluten, I started to feel better. My foggy mind began to clear, my gas was less, and I didn't have daily headaches. I'd vacillate between eating and not eating bread and pasta. Mac and cheese was comfort food, so I often cheated. When we ate out if they brought bread to the table, I wanted it and I'd have a slice. I was eating a lot of animal products. Steak, eggs, milk, chicken, and deli meat. I wasn't eating lots of veggies and I didn't see a big increase in my energy levels. My acne didn't clear up.

While we were on our honeymoon, we had a huge fight. We had gone on a Caribbean cruise in March. I was six months pregnant. It was my first cruise and I just wanted to sleep. He was furious that I wanted to sleep all the time. I wasn't drinking any caffeine for fear it would harm the baby. He left the cabin, and I was exhausted from traveling, rocking, and arguing. I fell asleep. When I woke up, he still wasn't back. *I better go find him. I hope he is not drinking again.*

When I walked onto the lower deck, I looked up at the upper deck, there was a man holding a cigarette. I almost turned away; then I saw the hand. He was standing there smoking. I was frozen. *Janna, you are pregnant and married. There is nothing you can do. You made your bed; now you have to lie in it. Smoking is a gripping addiction; give him time.* I walked slowly back to the cabin. I felt depressed and defeated. I knew I failed. I had proof of his lies. *Now what?*

When he opened the door to our cabin, I was angry. "You smell like smoke!" I accused. He looked me square in the eyes and said, "I was playing the slots in the bar." with a shrug. "I saw you," I hissed. There was no response. He crawled into bed and closed his eyes. *I think this is my problem not his, he isn't upset I am. I am broken and need to figure my way out of this situation. Boundaries don't seem to be working but I don't understand why.*

While I was pregnant, I was part of a *Wellness for Mothers* program. A nun came to support and advise me. She would ask me about what I was eating and encourage me to add things to my diet. During my first trimester, I shared with her I was struggling to feel full. She encouraged me to eat oatmeal and peanut butter to help me stay full longer. This diet change did help me feel full for a sustainable amount of time. I ate both, with sugar.

We had our first son on June 10, 1997. Jordan's birth was scary; he had the cord wrapped around his neck, and the hospital staff was not kind or supportive. When he was born, he was purple from a lack of oxygen. After they made sure he was pink and breathing they handed him to me. They didn't allow me to hold him for more than a few seconds, and then they took him out of the room. I told Tom to stay with Jordan. The nurses helped me dress in a clean gown and left me alone in a dark room. I fell asleep.

I don't know how long I slept, but I woke up alone in a strange, dark room without my baby. It was horrible. I felt terror and panic. I can be stubborn or tenacious, so I stood up and walked out of the room. I was halfway down the brightly lit hall and started to blackout. I bent down and began to crawl toward the nurse's station. I was going to my baby. I felt dizzy, nauseous, and determined. A nurse found me and tried to convince me to return to my room. It was not going to happen.

She went and found Tom, and he helped me walk to Jordan. They were getting ready to feed him sugar water from a bottle so he would "perk up" from the sugar. I had read about this, and I told the nurse, "No!"

"It will help your baby."

"No! You are absolutely not giving my son sugar water for his first meal!" She argued with me, but I come from a dysfunctional family, and when I was adamant about something, especially my children, I didn't back down. I raised my voice and started to swear. My inner warrior was fierce. Another nurse arrived and intervened. She agreed I would breastfeed Jordan. Then he went back under the oxygen hood. That was when I became Jordan's mother. I had fought for what was best for us. I realized sometimes I must stand up for what I believe to experience serenity later.

Jordan changed my life and my understanding of love. When he was born, and I was holding him in my arms, I experienced a kind of love, a serenity I had never felt before. I looked into his blue eyes; *I will be the best person I can, I will protect you, I pray your life will always be happy and serene.* I knew the true purpose of my love for him would be to protect him and nurture him on a journey to becoming his greatest self. This is the true power of love.

Chapter Eighteen
Courage

I had heard a person describe courage as acting while feeling afraid. The definition I read was, "the ability to do something that frightens one." I was a courageous person, so I decided to continue to be courageous and recognize the fear. *I don't feel afraid much, interesting.* I needed courage to face life and make changes.

My relationship with my mom was one of the changes I experienced. After Jordan was born, I experienced love for my son and saw some of the great things my mom had done for me. I asked her questions; I called her more often and I wanted my child to know his grandmother. I had a different relationship with Tom, too. I knew I didn't love him in the way a wife was intended to love a husband. I didn't understand all our issues. However, there was no more denial that my lack of trust would one day end our marriage. *I just need to raise this son with him. I will not be a single mother. I must accept this as it is.*

I wasn't healthy enough to face separation, but I realized I wasn't attached, so I tried to figure out how to survive in my marriage. My conflicting thoughts were fueling an inner war. Jordan was my peace.

Jordan had the brightest smile with one dimple on his left chubby cheek. I loved his bright, happy blue eyes; I loved his precious hands and feet. I loved the way he absorbed everything around him. Living life with a young child and an insecure marriage was hard. The blessing was Jordan was an excellent baby. He didn't cry much, and he was happy most of the time. I sang and talked to Jordan constantly. I used some sign language with him. When we were in the car, I would sing; when we were at home, I would talk and sing to him. "A-B-C-D-E-F-G" His big blue eyes would look at me. He had a beanie bird, and I thought it would sound like Road Runner. I would say, "meep, meep," and poke its soft nose into him. I would make it fly around him and sing and dance.

In some baby books about introducing food to a new eater, I read they recommended I start with cereal, then move to veggies, and lastly add in fruit. I read sweet flavors were added last, and sugar was not a good idea, especially for a new eater.

My mom bought me a small food grinder. I would cook for Tom and me and then mash our veggies to feed Jordan. It saved me time and money to make my baby food. I bought premade baby food for nights when we ate out or I wasn't cooking. Then, I was able to wash the jars and use them to store extras from the previous night's meals.

After Jordan was born, my acne became egregious. No matter what I did, I couldn't get the acne under control. I was exhausted and didn't have the energy to prepare food. I slipped back into my old habits of eating high-sugar, high processed foods. I still stayed off gluten for the most part, but I would cheat, bread was easy to grab and eat. My habits were affecting my health again. We ate boxed food or ate out constantly. I started to deteriorate, and I struggled with the same issues as before. Headaches, constipation, and gas, and now I had acne too. *I must eat differently. I felt better when I ate raw vegetables and fruits.* I thought.

Habits are powerful, and change can be difficult. I did my best to make better choices, but I felt alone and exhausted. Tom worked long hours, I took on everything with the household and I worked. I didn't have a good balance. It all felt like work.

When I was young, I took on the responsibility of cleaning, laundry, and getting myself and my brother ready and on time for events. Control gave me the illusion of security. *If everything on the outside is neat and clean, then I know I will be okay.*

As a new mother, I was responsible for everything in Jordan's world. I was terrified I would make huge mistakes, and I had no real experience with babies. I was addicted to control, and it was destroying my joy. I wouldn't ask for or accept help from anyone. When they tried, I was harsh and critical. Control is a destructive and corrosive behavior. It's fatal to any healthy relationship.

Jordan was a normal child and was waking up a couple of times a night, to be fed and have his diaper changed. When I didn't get enough sleep, all my worst traits were magnified. I was struggling in my body, my mind, and my spirit. I realized life requires courage, and I was going to be as courageous as I could be. I was motivated by my love for Jordan. I didn't want him to struggle the way I had.

Chapter Nineteen
Wisdom

After a year with wisdom as my focus, I thought, *I have none. We all have wisdom; I support you being open to yours.* My healthy voice reminded. The Serenity Prayer says "the wisdom to know the difference" between what I can change and what I cannot change. I questioned *Does my ability to change something only apply if I have the power?* I thought of my Grandma Alice and Grandpa Carl as being wise. *Does a person have to get older to obtain wisdom?*

I tried to imagine where I had wisdom; I thought about my natural abilities, like organizing. I believed I had wisdom in the world of organizing. *No one ever taught me how I just know. Is wisdom better than knowing?* I looked up the definition of wisdom, the quality of having experience, knowledge, and good judgment. From this definition, my grandparents had experience, I had the knowledge about organizing, and I knew I would need to work on good judgment. *Does experience lead to knowledge and good judgment?*

Jordan was an incredible child. He was curious and absorbed everything around him quickly. I talked, signed, and sang to him constantly. He started talking at six months old and by one, he was putting simple sentences together. He also sang to me before he could talk.

I remember going to the grocery store; he was sitting in the child's seat. We were in the aisle with all the cereal and he wanted a specific kind of cereal. "What do you want?" I asked him. He repeated the words, but I still didn't know what he was asking for. I took him out of the seat and let him walk around in the aisle; I was hoping he could point to what he wanted. He walked up and down the row of all the colorful boxes, and he picked Life. I knew that wasn't the word he was saying, though.

Later, he was able to say, "rucky karms" and I finally understood he was asking me for Lucky Charms. I appreciated his patience with me and bought him a huge box. He picked out the marshmallows, ate them, and left the cereal. I figured that gave him less sugar and I fed the cereal bits to Tom. When he opened the box, a huge laugh came bursting out of him. Then he teased Jordan about eating the best parts. Together they picked through the left cereal and found a few missed marshmallows. We still call it Rucky Karms.

I didn't have much wisdom. My wisdom was really survival, but I was able to learn to pause and use good judgment more often. That was a wise practice indeed.

Chapter Twenty
Feelings

The definition of feelings I used here was energy in the body and mind; it can be observed or experienced as shape, color, and location in the body. Learning to be connected to my feelings and my body was a process that required many years and much practice. The dividends paid have been incredible congruency and clarity in my life.

In early October, my mom called "Janna."

"Hi, Mom, what's up?"

"I am headed to be with my Dad. His cancer has spread throughout his body, and he is in the hospital. They have him on a morphine pump; it looks like this may be the end."

"Oh damn," I said numbly. I slid down the wall. The room spun around me. "I will call you when I have more news." She said. "Okay, I love you, mom." I hung up the cordless phone and set it on the floor next to me. I laid my head against my knees and didn't move for a long time. *Why can't I cry? This man is one of the most important people in my life. It will come; remember you're patient, Janna.*

My feelings were not safe in my childhood; I would float to the ceiling if I had feelings. *I am an adult; why don't I feel this grief? You're broken; you are not capable of really loving anyone.* I judged.

Grandpa Carl getting ready to cross over was unimaginable to me. I know today I was numb and in shock. Grief feelings go through cycles. Shock was my first feeling. Shock spares me from the brutal pain and suffering to know I will never experience the human connection with that person again. I only felt my feelings during significant, dramatic events like the car accident. I wasn't able to talk about my feelings at these times; I knew I had them, though. It seemed like I had a delay in when I felt them, though it was often weeks after an event when I was free thinking that the feelings would come. Mostly, I didn't have names for them. Feelings were good or bad.

My beloved Grandpa died on October 20, 1999. I was devastated and didn't know how to grieve the loss. I knew my life would never be the same again.

The two people I knew loved me, I could always trust, were together on the other side. Heaven is where there is no battle to be fought in my head, no suffering. I could be with Grandma Alice and Grandpa Carl. I wish I was there with them, at peace.

When Jordan was two and a half, I was still in denial about my addiction to control, and I was suffering from the consequences. I had been sober for about eight years, and I experienced an emotional bottom. I had prayed to have my physical obsession with alcohol removed years earlier.

That is all God can do for me, I falsely believed.

I continued to work on my mental health, but I had done no work to be connected with my feelings or address my beliefs and thoughts. I hit an emotional bottom. I knew I needed help and had to ask for it.

In November, I had gone to a sober women's gathering and risked being vulnerable with the women. It was tough to open up and trust all of those women, but I was suffering. We were all sitting in a large circle, and I knew most of them pretty well. We had gathered at my mentor's home. It was a big house on a hill overlooking a Pennsylvania valley. It had big windows and a large down-sloping grass backyard. There was no fence; it was open and a lush green grassy lawn.

"I need help." I squeaked through my tight throat. "I am constantly tired, angry at Tom, and trying to control everything," I admitted. "Tom asks me if he can help, and I snap at him, and then he just leaves because I am so mean to him. I need help." I say again.

"I don't know how to trust anyone, including myself," I explained. When I do trust a person, they often are not honest with me, and I get hurt; it's my pattern, and I have no clue how to change it," I admitted to these women. I focused on myself and didn't blame others but had no grace or love toward myself.

The women all shared what they were experiencing in their lives, and my mentor talked about a place called The Caron Foundation. She had gone there recently for the week-long co-dependency program.

I'm not co-dependent and can never leave Jordan for a whole week. I thought.

During the gathering, my mentor suggested I reach out to The Caron Foundation, where I could get help. I called them. Then, I spent a week learning about my feelings, self-love, and how to work through the trauma from my youth. I started to come out of denial about how my parents' alcoholism had affected me.

The Caron Foundation was a youth addiction treatment center with a weeklong family treatment program. Caron Foundation addresses overall behavioral health, treating Co-occurring disorders and substance use disorders, with residential programs for teens, young adults, adult men, adult women, and older adults. The counselors taught me to identify four feelings and give safe feedback to others. They took me through a meditation to help me reconnect with my inner child, and they set the stage for me to see how I had been hurt and could heal. It was exactly what I needed to begin inner healing toward congruency, acceptance, and love. It was a busy week.

I was there with about eighteen people, and then we worked in smaller groups of six, four, and one. As I write this, the word "we" is natural when I describe Caron because I didn't feel alone there. That was a powerful first. I felt seen and heard by the staff and the other attendees. I worked hard to remain open, vulnerable, and be seen. I trusted them and was letting go of fear and control.

They gave me the start toward belonging to myself, and they helped me begin to identify the shame I felt growing up. I learned not to blame my parents. They did the best they could. I also learned to recognize the events that I played over and over in my head as trauma. My traumatic childhood shaped my need to control, blame, and criticize myself. I learned that I rarely used feeling words to identify my feelings. I did use cliches and judgments.

The Caron Foundation opened my eyes to my past, my feet to my present, and my heart to my future. I feel deep gratitude for my experience. It was the beginning of emotional healing on a core level. It was the beginning of becoming comfortable with myself and healing from my traumatic childhood. The Caron councilors suggested I start with four feelings: sad, happy, mad, afraid. They started simply. When they asked me how I felt, I constantly gave them words of judgment. During a group setting, the therapists took us on a meditation journey.

"Okay, everyone take three deep breaths," she guided.

"Imagine walking through a forest, down by a stream, up a hill, and out to a large meadow. Then, you find a large rock, sit down, and relax. As you are relaxing, a small child approaches. You look at the child and think it looks familiar. Then, when the child gets closer, you see that it is you. The child takes your hand, and you walk to your house together. As you get to the house, you walk up to the door."

I was sitting on a chair, holding a big stuffed bear. I could feel the terror in my brain and body as the therapist brought me to the red house in North Dakota. I didn't want to go into the house.

I began to cry hard. *I can't go into that house.*

I imagined looking at the little girl; she shook her head with a silent "no." I heard the therapist say, "You can bring something in with you to keep you safe." I imagined a substantial brown grizzly bear at my side. He was holding my other hand. When we opened the front door, I ran to the bathroom and closed myself in, alone again.

I could hear the therapist speaking, but I was huddled in the bathroom with the door locked. The therapist finished the meditation, and I was sobbing, with massive tears falling on the stuffed bear's head.

The therapist asked, "Would you like to do some work?" I reply with a nod. *Yes.*

"Janna, how are you feeling?" The therapist asked me.

"Like there is a lead ball in my stomach."

He smiles softly with encouragement.

"Can you pick a word on the list?" I look at the list. There is a plain white sheet of paper with large letters that read.

SAD

HAPPY

MAD

AFRAID

"I feel sad," I said after a long pause. It was a challenge, but I was motivated to learn about my feelings. I had to change my judgments into identifiable feelings. I had to pause and think about what I felt and try to give the feelings a name. I was slow and struggled to identify my feelings.

This practice of connection with my feelings was the beginning of real healing and staying present and attached to myself. The Caron staff taught me this sentence:

I feel __ when__.

For Example, I feel sad when my brother hits me. I feel mad when I am left alone. I feel happy when I am hugged.

This simple, concise sentence changed my ability to express and communicate my feelings to others. I learned a new way to talk about my feelings. It took a commitment on my part to practice. I practiced over and over again. I taught it to the people in my life and practiced with them, too. The therapist explained, "It's also important not to say "when you" or "when someone" as that becomes a blaming sentence.

For example: "When you __ it makes me angry." Versus "I feel angry when I see you smoking."

In the first example, I am blaming the smoker for my anger. The phrase "makes me" implies blame. In the second sentence, I own "seeing them smoke," and I feel angry. I'm being accountable for my feelings. Being responsible for myself is healthy. When I'm critical, controlling, and responsible for others, it's codependent or *counter dependent*.

The Caron Foundation taught me to provide safe feedback to others without judgment or shame. This process is called mirroring. Here are two examples of how to use mirroring:

"I see you are (state exactly what I am seeing) twisting your wedding ring while you talk about your husband/wife/partner." And "I heard you say (Then repeat as close to what I heard them say as I can) your husband/wife/partner is an incredible person."

Mirroring is a fact-based reflection with no judgment; as the mirror, I use my senses to reflect what I see and hear. It allows the communicator to reflect on their own communication or actions. Then, they have the power to determine if it's accurate or not and amend or repair the information if it's inaccurate. Finally, it empowers the communicator to evaluate the information. This is empowering because it's a solution they own. Each of us knows every detail about our own lives. The solution is born from an internal connection and wisdom. When I'm empowered to create my own solutions, I'm more successful and tend to work through an issue more quickly with less suffering. I know everything about myself and my story. When I hear it mirrored back to me, I can think through my history and come up with the best solution.

It felt unexciting and dull when I started using this technique to support others. Then I realized it keeps the power out of my hands. It keeps me from controlling or manipulating their solution. *It doesn't feel exciting. What a gift.*

I love using this technique in my life. I have seen friends and family resolve deep-rooted wounds when they hear their own words repeated back to them.

While at Caron, during my one-on-one, I told my counselor, "Codependency doesn't match my behaviors." My counselor smiled kindly and said, "Janna, you're not codependent; you're counter dependent."

Huh? I had never heard of counter dependency. My definition of my counter dependency is self-reliance. I trust no one and make up black-and-white rules to navigate my life. Isolation and control give me the illusion I'm safe.

Learning about counter dependency changed my awareness of my behaviors. I realized I decided not to rely on or trust other people. I realized I had gone to any length not to feel my feelings. I used manipulation, punishment, and control in relationships to get my needs met and avoid intimacy. I was rigidly self-sufficient. I made boundaries with others to control them. I would take control and depend on only myself. I didn't ask for help or share responsibility with others. These are some of my traits.

This thinking helped me survive my traumatic childhood. I learned my independence was a tool for my protection growing up in my family. While these behaviors had kept me safe in my dysfunctional family, they hurt me and the people who tried to love me as an adult. They kept me isolated and alone. Feeling safe nurtured my denial about the destruction of my controlling behaviors.

I was responsible for changing my behaviors.

I had developed them as a powerless child, but they didn't support the person I wanted to become as an adult.

After treatment at Caron, it was recommended I get a therapist. I had several therapists before, but none I trusted. I had a traumatic experience with a therapist in college. She shared personal information about herself during group sessions. She held a session where the group gave feedback to each other without guidelines. There was no safety structure, as in the communication tools I learned at Caron. The feedback I received felt like criticism, judgment, and shaming. I felt betrayed and was deeply hurt by this session. I wasn't eager to get a therapist.

Then I met Ken. A friend had mentioned a new therapist who moved to the area and was accepting new clients. I had a negative experiences with women therapists, so I decided to move forward. I would try to trust just a little.

"Hi, My name is Ken; welcome to my office. Please sit down and make yourself comfortable."

Ken was in his fifties, balding slightly, and had kind blue eyes. He wore a cotton button-up, collared light blue shirt with khaki pants. The room had quiet lighting, a wooden desk, a couch, and a chair.

I sat on the couch and put the small pillow on my lap in front of my stomach. "What brings you here today?"

"Well, I went to The Caron Foundation for the Family program, and they told me I needed to get a therapist when I was back home." Then I took a breath. Ken did, too.

"Okay." He paused and looked into my eyes. "Is there anything else you would like to tell me?" *Wow, he wants me to tell him more. He is looking at me and asking me to tell him more. Wow.*

"Sure, my therapist there told me I am counter dependent. I think I am, too. Caron taught me I use judgment in place of my feelings. I also want you to know I was hurt by a therapist when I was in college."

"So, correct me if I am wrong here, but I hear you telling me you think you might be counter dependent, you're doing some work on your feelings, and you had a bad experience with a therapist while you were in college. Is that accurate?" I remember leaving the first session feeling heard. *I think I can trust him, and he will help me on my journey.* He was a miracle in my life.

Ken used a therapy tool called EMDR (Eye Movement Desensitization and Reprocessing). It's a comprehensive psychotherapy in which experiences preserved as disturbing when recalled are processed to resolution using bilateral stimulation such as eye movement. It has been found effective in therapy with people with post-traumatic stress disorder (PTSD). It took Ken and me two sessions to document the memories and the trauma I had experienced in my life. Then we got to work.

"Okay, Janna, can you tell me about your earliest memory that you think about often."

I pause, then remember the voice of Ed McMahon, "Heeeeerrrrrreeeeeeee's Johnny," I tell him the story of getting out of bed and sitting on my dad's lap.

"We are both drinking his beer," I state.

"Okay, and how old are you in this memory?" He asks with a neutral tone.

"Um, I think I'm three," I say.

"Okay, that is good, Janna; let's go to the next memory."

"The next memory is in Iowa; we lived by water."

"What kind of water?"

"I am not sure."

"Okay, what do you remember about this memory?"

"My brother doesn't want me tagging along with him."

"Is your brother older or younger? What's your brother's name?"

We volley back and forth until he has a timeline with documented memories. He now has the most complete history of my memories and trauma.

Then he says, "Let's find out which method will work best for you." He hands me a set of headphones. I place them on my head. He has a remote with a volume dial, or maybe it controls the speed; I am not sure. He turns it on, and I hear a click. Then I see him turn up the dial, I hear a "beep" in my right ear "beep" in my left ear. It moves back and forth.

"Can you still hear me?" he asks. "yes," I say. He starts asking me questions about my "Heeeeaaarrrrssss Johnny memory." *This beeping is not good. If I tell him, he may not be able to help me, or he may get mad. It feels like hard work to hear him, probably because I have to listen so closely when I'm interpreting. I need to tell him.* He gets a few questions into the memory, and I say, "I'm sorry, but this beeping in my ears bothers me. I listen for a living, and I think it's just too much."

"Oh, okay," he holds out his hand; I remove the earphones. *He's not mad at me. That's different.* "Do you want to try the eye movement or paddles you hold?"

"Um, paddles?" He hands me two black, semi-flat oval objects. "Place one in each hand, please."

I separated the paddles and put one in each hand. He has another remote with a dial. He turns them on, and I feel a pulse in one and then the other. It flows back and forth between the two.

He starts asking me questions again. "So, you were saying you would hear the TV, creep out of bed, and look in the room to see if your dad was there alone." *Wow, that was without any trauma; I am starting to trust this man.*

We had begun a process that would continue for years. I noticed that as we worked, my memories became more precise; I remembered how the water moved and flowed, then remembered it was a creek, stream, or river. The memories also began to change. As I worked on earlier memories, some of the older memories no longer felt like trauma. I realized I had started to categorize trauma in my mind like office boxes on a shelf. They had labels such as unwanted, unlovable, broken, and failure. It would contain the traumas when I didn't think or believe I was cared for.

My rational brain joined with my emotional brain, and all the pages from the boxes were sorted through, read, acknowledged, and resolved. When the rational brain was connected, I could understand more about the memory on each page in each box; they were no longer charged with trauma energy.

When I thought about Sean not wanting me at the river, I realized he was a young boy expected to take care of his younger baby sister near dangerous moving water. I imagined how stressful and scary that might have been for him. Plus, I kept walking away from him. I no longer felt hurt or unwanted. It was replaced with a new perspective and compassion for my brother.

Ken also taught me how to begin a difficult conversation with the words "I imagine." He helped me realize I don't know what others think and feel, so I learned to say, "I imagine __." Then, "Is that accurate?" or "Does that sound accurate?"

I sometimes hear what people have said incorrectly, and getting their corrections is rewarding. I enjoy feeling heard when people connect with me in this way. Having these communication tools calmed my anxiety and helped me communicate better with Tom, my kids, and the people in my life. I remember it felt awkward and rehearsed in the beginning. *People are going to get irritated that I'm constantly saying these same things over and over. They will think I'm not authentic.* I thought. They never told me if they did. I started to see real trust and connection with my female friends and began to experience less judgment toward people. My internal thoughts began to be more curious. *I wonder how things are going for* __, I would think. This all takes time and practice. Consistent practice became a habit. It's worth it!

Tom and I became pregnant a second time and lost the baby. I suspect it may have been because of the gluten I was consuming. I read about the connection between Celiac and infertility, and it answered the questions I had about times in my drinking when I could have become pregnant but didn't. I was struggling to avoid the easy go-to food of bread specifically. I felt cheated that I couldn't enjoy what I wanted to eat without consequences.

I'm only going to eat just a little bit of bread occasionally, but as soon as I ate a little, I'd crave more. *I am responsible for losing this baby; it's all my fault.* I didn't know how to share my sadness and thoughts with Tom. I was alone because I couldn't open up to him or trust him.

Ken helped me see I needed to grieve for my loss. I bought a picture of a beautiful hydrangea flower with a gold frame. The flower was purple and periwinkle and different shades of blue. That was how I honored this child. I think of her whenever I see a hydrangea bush. *If this is all my fault, then I have the power to change it. I am getting gluten out of my diet.* I bought another Atkins cookbook and started to get serious about getting gluten out of my diet for good.

On December 12, 1999, Tom bought me a Christmas gift, and he was so excited he didn't want to wait for Christmas. "Janna, your gift is ready, and you'll love it. Can I give it to you today?" he said with joy and excitement on his face. Once he bought the gifts, he wanted to give them to us. He usually did his Christmas shopping on December 24.

The gift was a second ring to wear with my wedding ring, which had three diamonds on a band. It had the matching swoosh as my wedding ring.

I had been doing so much feeling work with my mind and body connection, and I knew I was pregnant the moment it happened. I felt the heat spreading in my body. It was like when a pebble strikes the surface of the water. I looked at him and said, "I'm pregnant."

He said, "I hope so!" We were so excited when we received confirmation of this pregnancy.

Chapter Twenty-One
Honesty

The definition of honesty, according to Webster's Dictionary, is adherence to the facts. "Just the facts, ma'am" (Dragnet). *This should be easy. Will it? Yes, I am an honest person. Are you too honest?*

Anytime my inner addict uses the word "should," I am cautious. Should is a shaming word. It's the word that denies things as they are. Denial can be the opposite of acceptance, and honesty can be blurred without acceptance. A good friend once said, "I no longer should on myself."

During my third pregnancy, I was nauseated all day during the first trimester. I read a book about natural childbirth, which mentioned the hormone-activated olfactory system (heightened smell) as the possible cause of morning sickness. The suggested solution was lemon. I smelled it, ate it, and drank it in my water all day for weeks. It did seem to help with my nausea. I talked with my first mentor after she had experienced a home birth, and she recommended a book called *Alternative Birth Methods*. The book described having a natural water birth. As I was reading about how easy it is for a baby to move from fluid to fluid and the easier manageability of the contractions in gravityless water, I was convinced. I wanted to experience a water birth at home.

I found a midwife in a neighboring town trained in water births. I read everything I could find on the subject. I watched videos and did all I could to make it happen. The trained midwife was on board, but the catch was that the hospital didn't support this idea entirely. They had laboring tubs but didn't support women having babies in the water. The midwife told me we might set it up if the timing worked. I kept telling myself it would happen. Then, the midwife left the medical office where I was seeing her. I arrived for my checkup, and they told me she was no longer employed there. I was devastated. I left there in shock.

How am I going to have this baby without her support? We prepared for this; she told me she would support me. Why didn't I get her number? Does she have my number?

I felt afraid and powerless. I needed to remain honest with myself. *It's going to be okay.* My healthy voice chimed in.

A few days later, the midwife called me, and she and I met and made the final arrangements for me to give birth at home in a birthing tub. It would work out and be even better than I had hoped.

My mom found a birthing tub company online that rented equipment for home births. The company sent the blowup tub, an electric heater, a long tube to attach to a faucet that allowed us to fill and empty the tub, and a huge plastic liner. There were detailed instructions about how and when to assemble it and how to clean, dismantle it, and send it back to the company.

My plan scared Tom, but he showed up and supported what I wanted fully. I'm grateful to him for supporting my vision. We had been told we were having a boy, and in May, Tom picked the name Dylan after Bob Dylan, one of Tom's favorite musicians.

In early June, I was standing in the dining room of our open living area, ironing a dress for a friend's baby shower. Tom was playing on the floor with Jordan; a Bob Dylan DVD was playing. "I love the name Dylan. What about a middle name?" I asked,

"Thomas," Tom exclaimed. I paused, looked up, and said, "Dylan Thomas! I love it!"

My mom had flown in a few days before the birth so she could be there and help with any last-minute needs. As my labor began, I felt calm and relaxed; I was happy to remain at home for labor and the birth. "Janna, do you want me to fill the tub now?" Tom asked from the kitchen.

"I think so," I replied.

"Your contractions are 10 minutes apart; it's time." my mom added. I looked at my mom's face, and she was excited.

I looked at Tom standing at the sink. He looked fearful and nervous. When our eyes met, I winked at him. "We got this," I said, reassuring him. "My body was designed for this." I reminded him.

I had Tom and Jordan, my mom, the midwife, a nurse friend, our Physician's Assistant and her daughter, my spiritual mentor, and her daughter, all there to love and support us. The midwife brought supplies from another midwife who assisted the Pennsylvania Amish community. The support of an entire village was there to help and support us. Dylan was born in our home in a birthing tub. We did it.

One of my primary reasons for having a baby at home was so Jordan could participate at whatever level he chose. I had talked to him about Dylan coming, and he had participated during the pregnancy. He had heard Dylan's heartbeat and asked a few questions while I was in labor. He was free to play in his room, come in and check on me, and go back to playing. At one point, he asked me, "Where are the fish?" and "Are you okay, Mom?"

"Yep, this is the hard part I told you about, and I am okay." He patted my head and bounced back into his room. Where he stayed for most of my labor, he only came out to see when I was actively pushing. My mentor held him, and she lovingly answered any questions he had. We all provided him with love, answers, and support throughout the process. He knew he belonged with our family. Jordan was present to welcome his new baby brother into this world.

My labor was manageable. I was able to relax, float, and rest between contractions. I'd catch my breath, and my body didn't feel the intensity of the contractions in the same way as a dry birth.

The midwife asked me to stand up, out of the water, a few times to check the position of Dylan's head. When I stood, the weight of my protruding midsection was cumbersome and forceful. Standing was difficult, and I felt enormous and heavy until I was back in the water again.

"Okay, Janna, you are ready to push now."

I looked up, "Really? Now, it's time?"

"Yep!" She replied cheerfully. I was shocked; I thought I had hours left. I still felt energy in my body and mind; I wasn't depleted and exhausted as I had been with Jordan's birth. I gave a few hard pushes, and Dylan floated out into the water. I brought him up to my body and snuggled him close without bringing him into the air. Dylan opened his eyes and looked at me through the water.

"Janna! Is it a boy or a girl?" my mom exclaimed.

I looked down and brought him up out of the water, "Well," I said as I looked into his eyes, "shall we tell them, Dylan Thomas?"

The room "oohed" and "aahed" when they heard his name. All our eyes were moist, and there was a bright energy of love and unity. After I nursed Dylan for the first time, my spiritual mentor, friend, and their daughters guided me into the shower and washed me. They all shared with me what the experience was like for them. They gave me the gift of physical nurturing and shared their joy at being a part of our story. I was cared for, and I trusted these women. I'm filled with love and joy as I write about it. I'll always be grateful for these women and our shared time together before, during, and after Dylan's birth.

The two daughters present were both at turning points in their lives, and my friends shared with me how the experience for them shaped how they felt about their bodies, their future, and childbirth. These were intimate moments, and I feel warmth in my heart when I remember them. Jordan never experienced his parents leaving him and bringing home a new baby. He was a part of the experience, and he, too, was embraced by love and support.

This was the best, most empowering event of my life, and I think it might qualify me as a real hippy, too. I was the first person to hold my son, and he went into the arms of my mom. Tom and Jordan held him together. Dylan didn't cry for two days. Strangers never held him. He was loved, nurtured, and welcomed into this world by his family and friends.

As I moved through this experience, I stayed honest with myself about how I had been affected by being in the hospital with Jordan. His birth was a trauma for me. I did the best I could, and I learned more about myself with Jordan's birth. I tried to share my experience with Tom.

I had been told that honesty without compassion can be hurtful. I maintained compassion for Tom's fear about the decision to choose home birth. I heard him when he shared his fears, and we discussed them. Ken taught us the idea of two "yeses" and a "no." This means that when a couple makes a decision, if there are two "yeses," it's a green light.

If there is one "no," then the light is red. Tom agreed to the home birth; we had two "yeses." Ultimately, my honesty with him led him to support my decision reluctantly.

Chapter Twenty-Two
Willingness

I define willingness as open, ready, and thinking about the action I need to take. Acceptance of what is. Willingness gives me a pause and a breath. It allows me time and space to think about what will come next. Sometimes, willingness is easy; for example, I'm willing to get a raise. Sometimes, willingness is difficult, like when I go to the dentist. Sometimes, willingness is impossible. I'm willing to eat meat. (nope!) The pause is good for me because of my controlling personality and childhood trauma. I need a pause to think, breathe, and prepare to respond. Responding is better than reacting.

As my boys grew older and I continued therapy, I was still struggling with the habit of eating the way I had in my youth. I was feeding my children too much fast food. It was easy to drive to McDonald's, Wendy's, and Burger King and capitalize on a free toy for a few minutes of peace while I drove home from the babysitter's house. Plus, I didn't enjoy cooking, so it felt like self-care not being on the hook to cook.

When Dylan was a toddler, he was not interested in eating meat. I falsely believed it was required to stay healthy. He loved "dippy sauce," so ranch, ketchup (the purple one), and honey became regular additions to our plates. Dylan didn't know ketchup was red until he was about five. I often bribed him with honey to eat a couple of chicken nuggets. I also feed them a lot of boxed, bagged, and canned food.

I found a farmer's market I liked and enjoyed being around all the farmers. There were organic fruits and vegetables we wanted. It was social, natural, and comforting for me to be among the farmers. It reminded me of being with my grandparents.

I didn't feel confident in the kitchen cooking, so I didn't invest much time in our food preparations and meal planning. I'd give the kids raw fruits and veggies with dippy sauces to eat. It was healthy, quick and easy.

While at Caron, I realized how important it was to understand and express my feelings. I came home with a page of feeling words. There were faces with expressions on them above each word. I placed it on the refrigerator and started looking at it while preparing fruits and veggies. I talked to the kids about it, too. I'd ask my kids, "What are you feeling?" Then we talked about it together. I hoped they'd grow up knowing their feelings. It was hard and awkward at first. Sometimes, I didn't have a word connected to my feelings.

While working with my therapist, in the beginning, I learned to pause and move my attention inward. My initial thoughts were typically judgments. Sometimes I'd say, "I don't know." Then he'd ask, "Where do you feel it?" I would answer, "In my guts."

Then he'd ask, "What color is it?" I would answer. "Black."

Finally, "What shape is it?" I would answer, "The shape of a large rock."

Then, sometimes, I could name it "inadequate." When I became better at naming my feelings, he still asked me where, what, and what. This practice helped me be connected to myself.

While I was at home, I would study the faces to figure out my feelings. I would ask myself how the pictures were different from each other and how they felt for me. I would try to remember when I felt worried, then think about where I felt it and its color and shape.

Today, I know how to identify my feelings and where they appear in my body. Stress is in my neck and shoulders. Shame starts in my chest and spreads out, sometimes downward and sometimes all around like a ripple in a pond. Anger is in my head. Hurt or fear is always under my anger and in my stomach. Disappointment is in my throat. Fear is deep in my bowels. Excitement and anxiety move throughout my body. Happy is in my head, and joy is in my chest. Joy and love are often similar in location, but shapes and colors differ. Now I understand the difference between shame and guilt, mad and angry, scared and afraid.

I am blessed to know sign language. This physical language has helped me develop a better understanding of my feelings. I have invested years of practice in identifying my feelings at this level with this clarity. Anger is a feeling I had in my childhood. The understanding was it had to be directed against the world. Anger is powerful. It's a hit of adrenaline.

At Caron, I learned that I was hurt and afraid under all my anger. I know I must do the work to understand my hurt or fear when I feel angry.

Shame is the feeling I am bad, broken, or not good enough. I can feel shame from myself, or I can feel shame from others toward me. Guilt is when I make a mistake; I now understand it's about my behavior. Then, I can make amends and change my behavior. It's the difference between *I am a mistake* and transitioning my beliefs to *I made a mistake*.

My shame has changed as I heal and connect with myself. In the beginning, all my shame was a black spiral beginning in my heart and moving downward. When I feel shame from my own judgement, it stings at my heart and explodes with black heat, moving outward. When others shame me, I feel a heavy black weight from my heart, spiraling toward my stomach. I am learning to understand these body cues. When I recognize it was shame from another person, I can respond. Then I take a deep breath and say, "Please do not shame and blame me."

The next hurdle to learn is remaining loving and kind toward others. I often want to react and punish them. I am working on finding grace and forgiveness when someone shames me today. There is no black-and-white rule here, and I can decide how to respond to the experiences in my life today.

Mad begins in my head, and it often comes from my thoughts. Angry starts below my ribs, and it moves out of me. Scared is at my heart. It's sudden and moves fast, like the wings of a hummingbird. Afraid comes on slowly. It creeps in and stays.

I know for me, the opposite of love is shame and indifference. One is an aggressive opposite, and the other is a passive opposite. I feel them both in my heart area. When I'm feeling shame, it overrides all other feelings. I'm more open and receptive to other feelings when I feel love. Falling in love feels vulnerable, addictive, and terrifying for me.

My feeling awareness has become more apparent as I practice staying connected to my emotions. Emotions are a body reaction coming from neurotransmitters and hormones. There is physical chemistry involved. Feelings come from thoughts and beliefs. I feel the need to repeat the first sentence in this paragraph: *my feeling awareness has become more apparent as I practice staying connected to my emotions.*

Love can be an emotion and a feeling. I can meet a person and feel a rush of warmth through my entire body. This is often called love at first sight. This would be an emotion. I can also spend time with a person, and as we are vulnerable, I start to think the person is kind, intelligent, and funny, and then I feel love in my heart.

Shame is an emotion when it comes at me from another person. It's based on their thoughts and beliefs that are shot my way like a slingshot. If I think and believe I deserve the shame, that's a double whammy of shame. I think this is why shame had so much power over me during most of my life. I struggled to see the difference between internal and external shame. I'm now learning to identify the differences because I have identified how they move in my body.

My friend recently told me about a feeling wheel. It has three layers of feeling words. The inner circle is simple. Similar to the paper on the wall at Caron. It includes happy, surprised, bad, fearful, angry, disgusted, and sad. I know for me, bad and good are judgments and not feelings. This is an excellent place to start, with many words to peruse. Learning to feel my emotions was a daunting job initially, but as I practiced, it was easier. This wheel seems like it will be helpful to my future practice.

Willingness in my life leads to feelings in the happy slice of the wheel. It encourages my curiosity, brings me hopefulness, and tugs at acceptance. I try to remain willing for the things I decide are important to me.

Chapter Twenty-Three
Beliefs

While doing all the feeling work and looking at concepts like honesty and willingness, I started questioning my beliefs about some things my dysfunctional family influenced. I wondered if my feelings could be changed if I changed my beliefs and thinking. It was an interesting idea and I wanted to take the year to explore it. While I was in therapy, Ken would ask me questions, and it often would shine a light on the dysfunctional beliefs I held.

"Janna, I hear you telling me that your grandmother was the only adult who watched and cared for you. I understand how much you loved her."

"Yes," I replied.

"Did you tell me she would nap for several hours on the couch every day?"

"Yes, but she was home still; I knew I could wake her up," I say, defending my beloved grandmother.

"Okay, I imagine that for you, that felt like she was still watching you?"

"Definitely," I say stubbornly.

"How would you feel if you woke her up?"

"I never woke her up."

"Why not?"

"Because she was sleeping."

"Was she available while she was sleeping?" He asks neutrally. "Sure, but I see your point," I admit.

"I learned that a person who naps every day might be displaying symptoms of depression or ill health. Do you think she was depressed or sick?"

"Ummm, no, I think in the Clark family, as we get older, we nap every day. We all have low blood pressure." I responded.

"I see. Could she be watching you while she was asleep?"

"I guess she was not exactly watching us; she was just available if we needed her," I explain.

Ken was helping me see how I believed Grandma was watching me when, in truth, she was asleep. Grandma was an absent adult, too. He supported a shift in my judgment, guilt, and shame when I acted wrongly and there were no adults to guide and help me. *Is it possible that this is not my fault? Is it possible that if an adult were there watching us, it would not have happened?*

Yes. My inner wisdom answers. *Yes.*

I understood his point and was learning to recognize times in my youth when having a healthy, sober, awake adult would have changed the situation. I couldn't think of one time when I'd made a choice, then felt shame, and an adult was there for support and guidance. Not one. It was a dramatic shift in my evaluation of my youth. I took control and responsibility for everything, even at three years old. I could see how what I believed kept me safe and also kept me in self-shame and blame.

I don't blame my family; I know they were doing everything they were able to do. I am aware that a lack of resources, time, money, community, family, and mental health were at the root of the issue. I was also still grateful my grandparents were there for me as much as they could be. *Can you let yourself off the hook for your behaviors that bring you shame?* My healthy inner voice chimes in. *Not yet.* My critical voice replied.

When I felt afraid as a child, I would try to control my environment to feel safe. I was addicted to control in place of inner security and attachment. The way I learned to control myself was by using inner shame, and judgment was my bouncer. My inner thoughts were so negative and critical, which led to self-judgment without compassion; eating poorly, not exercising, and rejecting love from others were all tools I used against myself. I falsely believed this would aid my life. It allowed me to survive. I survived against impossible odds, and now I heard an inner voice that wanted to shine.

I knew I would spend the rest of my life evaluating my beliefs.

Chapter Twenty-Four
Values

When I could see how my beliefs needed to be reevaluated, I wanted also to evaluate my values. Values had to be the concrete the glass walls would be built on, not bricks this time, but glass windows so I could safely interact with the world. I was going to live in a greenhouse someday. I didn't value myself or my life, and I wasn't sure how I'd get there, but I knew I had to try. I began to look at values and how they shaped my choices. *What are the choices that support this value? What are the values that support this choice?* I questioned myself.

In 2003, I was interpreting for a deaf woman who worked for a government agency. A professor at a small local university came to see the deaf woman. The professor had lost her hearing in her twenties and was hoping to find help and support. During the meeting, we had decided to sit in a three-legged stool formation so the professor could read my lips. I offered to come and do some experimental interpreting for her during some of her classes. Then she revealed she had a PhD in nutrition and was the chair of the Nutrition Department. This was such a God thing. I wouldn't have independently looked for this opportunity, given my history with cooking, but it was the beginning of my curiosity about vegetarian food. It was also the beginning of questioning what I thought, believed, and valued about food.

One student was vegetarian; she was in a group of three for a lab class I would be interpreting. The three women all had a natural aptitude for cooking. The vegetarian was a thin, guarded woman with a natural radiant glow on her skin. I knew being a vegetarian meant she didn't eat meat. That was all I knew. As an interpreter, I was privy to conversations with the professor and the students. The vegetarian student never wore any makeup and looked beautiful with long, shiny hair and healthy-looking unpainted nails. I was curious about her.

I witnessed a lab class where the experiments were designed to teach different reactions between foods. The students were given instructions about how to mix the foods to observe the interactions. The vegan group labs were altered to be vegan. They used plant-based ingredients like almond milk, tofu, and butter without dairy.

The labs were designed to fail, but the plant-based group consistently succeeded. The food always tasted wonderful. I learned from watching them there were many options for vegetarians, and substitutions can be extremely effective for transitioning to a plant-based diet. These women had a relationship, a connection, with food that I intuitively knew I needed to learn about. I was curious and wanted to understand.

The professor walked between the countertop toward the vegan group, with me in tow. "Good morning, ladies" Do you have everything you need?"

"Yes, we have our almond milk, fruit, gluten-free flour, and egg replacer." They were making pancakes.

"Great, looks like you are all set to go; let me know if you need anything." The lab used baking powder and vinegar to give the pancakes a fluffy rise. I was already familiar with this trick from my Atkins waffles. It was fantastic to see the almond milk and vegan butter. This was when I learned that vegans don't consume dairy.

"Nothing with a face," she said. *Okay, that is confusing, most of my food had a face, I think. What about protein, she has to eat animals to get protein. Look at how glowy she looks; what am I missing?*

Each time they cooked it was delicious and successful. It gave me pause. I kept remembering her glowing, healthy appearance. I also saw a kind of prejudice from other people toward her and it made me look at my misconceptions about how I had been eating compared to how others ate.

When the students were done with the lab and it was all cleaned up, the vegan group would leave. Most of the time they finished before all the other groups. I often overheard the other students commenting on the same thing I had observed. The people studying sports nutrition would make comments on how their labs failed miserably and the veg group was successful. They were also trying to puzzle out the protein misconception and why the veg food always tasted good, looked good, and the women were done early. This group was innately competitive, and they seemed interested in winning. I could appreciate their comments, but I also wanted to think more deeply about where I had been wrong.

During the private meetings with the professor, I picked up on subtle pressure and disagreement from the professor toward the vegetarian to change her diet. "Professor, you are asking me to change values. I eat this way for my health, for the animals, and for the planet because I value all of these things."

"I'm just asking you to explore whether it's a healthy way to eat."

"I am in perfect health." After a pause, the student stood up and left the office. I heard her mention values, I too valued these things but didn't eat vegetarian. I became more curious.

In January 2004, I worked for a different university in the agriculture department. I Interpreted a class that was learning about genetically changed foods. They are called genetically modified organisms (GMO or GM). A few vegetarian students gave presentations about the negative aspects of GMOs. They talked about allergies, cancer, nutritional value, and environmental impacts. One student emphasized the social and ethical downside of GMs. I was interested in how few students were in support of GMOs. What they said made me think about the how and why of changed or engineered food. I'm a naturally curious person, and when something resonates with me, I'm inclined to do my own research and find answers to my questions.

I started to think about those memories of Grandpa Carl showing me how to test wheat. He had been involved in politics and was part of the 1643 Agricultural Act of 1961, which set up federal subsidies for grain farmers. I remembered a table conversation where he said, "My actions may have terrible consequences on the future of food in this country. They will affect the small farmers." He indicated his regret for his actions. He knew his intentions were honorable, but the results were possibly terrible for the future of food. I didn't understand everything he said at the time.

Food subsidies are a complicated business. The worst part is they put American food in the hands of politicians. The consequences are far-reaching and have almost destroyed small independent farming in America. Our food in America is in grave danger.

The family farm in Nebraska was the farm my mom grew up on. They primarily grew wheat on this farm, and I remember a huge vase filled with our wheat. It had a prominent place on a chair-side cabinet in the living room. I loved the feeling of the harvested grain running through my fingers. We all loved to touch the wheat berries and let them fall like water from our fingers. The wheat my grandpa grew in his field was the wheat he would plant back in the ground to grow future crops. This wheat was not genetically modified. My grandparents could rely on a previous crop to grow future crops.

These are now called heritage seeds. Most of the wheat crops in America are now genetically modified. Therefore, they cannot be used to plant for future harvests. They grow in the ground, but the soil no longer has proper minerals to support the nutrition in the wheat, and the seeds are infertile. These are consequences of government involvement and subsidies.

I learned to value fresh, natural food from my grandparents. I learned to value nature, and sunny weather, with some healthy days of rain. I grew up hearing the stories of my grandfather's involvement in politics and the ripples of his actions, positive and negative, on the future of food and our family legacy.

During this year, I changed very few beliefs, but the seeds were planted, and the remaining years gave me time and a willingness to challenge my beliefs when needed and solidify my values. I didn't value myself yet. However, my beginning value of the earth, the animals and my health had been evaluated and would be the foundation of learning to value myself.

Chapter Twenty-Five
Perspective

When I was young, I made observations, then made up what I didn't understand based on what I knew. I often made up what I thought was accurate. I asked my mom. "When will my breasts fall off?"

She paused, then said, "What?"

I knew she didn't understand, so I explained, "Well, Grandma Alice has one, so I am wondering when our breasts fall off?"

My grandmother only had one breast, and I could see her missing bump when she had on her pajamas. I must have lost some teeth by this time and puzzled out, on my own, when we are done with our breasts, they fall off like our teeth fall out. My mom explained, "Grandma had breast cancer, and they used surgery to remove her breast." I remember thinking, *how terrible. I liked my idea better.*

Perspective is an integral part of maturing. During the year, I focused on perspective. I learned to ask myself, *will another perspective help me work through this problem?* **The answer is yes.**

The boys had been exposed to Tom and I's love for hockey and their dad found an in-line hockey program at the local YMCA. In-line hockey is played on rollerblades and uses hockey equipment that is often lighter and smaller than its counterpart on ice. It's played on a composite tile surface. The rollerblades can grip while the puck moves smoothly across the tiles.

YMCA was building a youth program, so Tom signed them up right away. When he came home and told me, I was excited and anxious. It was an added activity to my busy schedule, and I was concerned about the cost. I had no idea that it would lead to some of my greatest joys in life.

We started taking the boys, and they loved it. The arena had a walking track around it, and I realized I could walk laps and watch them play at the same time. Tom was able to do some coaching so it was a win for the whole family.

We began to build a community of friends in a world we all loved. As a new program, they had kids of all ages playing together. Jordan and Dylan started to make friends, Tom was connecting with the other parents, and I exercised. It brought us all together in a healthy way. I imagine Tom saw how this would be positive for our family before I did. It became the one thing we all did together consistently for years. It brought many hours of joy and happiness to my life.

The practice of shifting my perspective was wonderful. When I shifted my focus from the cost of hockey to the time we would spend together, I realized the value of the experience.

One weekend, I went to the farmer's market and bought two quart-sized baskets of blueberries. When I arrived home, I took the berries and poured them into the basket. I owned a salad spinner, and it was a convenient way for me to wash and dry fresh fruit. I put the lid on the spinner and ran water over the berries while I spun them slowly and gently. I left them in the sink.

"Janna, can you come downstairs and help me for a minute?" Tom called from the basement. He was doing some woodworking in his shop downstairs.

"Sure, give me just a second, and I will be there," I replied.

I left the blueberries resting in the sink until they dried. Then, I planned to move them to a container in the fridge after I helped Tom.

When Tom and I were done about 20 minutes later, I came up the steps and walked into the kitchen. Dylan was sitting on the floor with the salad spinner between his legs. He was trying to hold the lid on to spin the blueberries. I imagined blueberry juice all over my kitchen.

"Oh, what are you doing with those blueberries, Dylan?" I said while trying to remain calm.

Dylan looked up at me with his big blue eyes and a determined look on his face and replied. "I am maken'um dizzy, so they don't know I'm eatin'em." I laughed and helped him spin them in the sink. From my perspective, the blueberries spun would be a disaster on the walls in the kitchen; from Dylan's perspective, he could eat them if they were dizzy. We were both right.

When I'm willing to see life from another person's perspective, no matter if I agree with it or not, I gain more grace, compassion, and love. *I hope I'll always be willing to shift my perspective so I can live in love with all people, not just the people I agree with. Perhaps if my new word is curiosity, I can learn more about becoming compassionate toward others.*

Chapter Twenty-Six
Curiosity

The definition of curiosity is a desire to know. I had looked at open-mindedness from 1994 to 1995, and I still had a critical, judgmental voice in my head. I thought I might need to practice being curious. *Judgment is not a bad thing. We pay people to be judges; without judgment, I would not have known I had a problem with alcohol.* It was when my judgment became morose, negative, and critical that it sabotaged my happiness and peace. I hoped exploring curiosity would help me become less critical.

Curiosity was a neutral place; it had no plan and no judgment. Its function was to obtain knowledge. I was learning about myself in new ways and with the practice of changing my perspective, I believed being curious could help with my critical negative thinking. *When my mind is curious, it holds a place for open-mindedness, learning, and magic. Curiosity lives in the moment.*

I was often uncomfortable meeting new people, and I noticed that I had strange behaviors that would pop up when I was around new people or in unfamiliar places. I felt nervous and would blurt out things without thinking them through. I judged myself harshly when this happened.

Through my curiosity, I have tried new foods, met new people, talked less, and learned more. *Curiosity lives in the moment.* In American Sign Language, the sign for *curious* is sometimes used before a question is asked. It's a bridge to discovery. *Curiosity for me comes from an open space, ready to be filled. I use meditation to create space. I use research to fill the space. Then when it is filled, I get to evaluate the information and prune what I keep and what doesn't work for me.*

The in-line hockey program was struggling, and Tom and I could see that our sons had a natural ability to be successful, and they enjoyed playing. He and I talked about transitioning them to ice hockey. The closest rink was 45 minutes away.

When I met Tom, he played hockey at this rink, and I had a dim memory of the arena with its dingy lighting and shabby carport covering. I remembered it was cold with nowhere to sit. We talked about the added hours and cost of new equipment for both boys. We decided that we would buy whatever they needed. We both felt that investing in hockey would be a good use of our resources, even though it might be a stretch. Hockey is an expensive sport.

I knew starting a new program would be uncomfortable for me. In evaluating my own discomfort, I thought trying new things might be a good focus for the next year.

Fall of 2006, we signed them up for ice hockey. The rink had been upgraded from the first time I was there with better lighting and metal bleachers. They had closed in the carport covering, so it blocked the outside weather. The entryway had lockers on the left down the hall, and the bathrooms and offices were to the right down another hall. The arena was straight through the second set of double doors on the opposite side of the entryway. The entryway had a huge hand-built stone fireplace that kept only the entryway warm. I loved that fireplace. The smell of the wood burning and the natural warmth of it was comforting after getting cold in the arena.

This hockey arena froze the ice from swamp coolers that were sitting on shelves in the corner. It made the temperature super cold. It created a very hard surface to skate on called fast ice. It allowed the metal skate blade to glide more easily and more smoothly across the surface. The slow ice gives you a better workout than fast ice, so we learned to appreciate slow ice, even though we didn't win any games.

They had to try out, and we bought the equipment they needed. Tom took them to free skates a couple of times, so they were able to transition from inline to ice, which is similar but requires a different technique. Tom worked with them, and they both picked it up very quickly. When I watched them, I could see they were both good skaters with great balance and physical skill.

I knew the rules of hockey and enjoyed strategy. When we went out to eat, we would talk about the rules, draw arenas on paper, and discuss the games. Jordan was extremely smart and seemed to pick up the concepts easily. Being three years older gave him a physical and intellectual advantage over Dylan, but Dylan was a natural and had his older brother to challenge him. His abilities were way ahead of any other kids his age.

They played on a team together for the first year. Tom helped coach. I made sure we were organized, had food, and had clean equipment. Hockey equipment reeks. Clean didn't mean it smelled good. I did some research about potential assistance with the cleaning and found out that tea tree oil would help gobble up the bacteria from sweat and body odor. I would wash the equipment with tea tree oil and then set it out in the sun to dry. This was the best approach at the time. Later, some wizard invented Febreze, and I added that to the "cleaning" routine.

Once again, we were making new friends and building a hockey community. Curiosity helped me stay engaged with other parents in the group, and I asked questions to learn more about everyone. This technique really worked well for me, and I knew all the families that came to the games. I also learned about the kids and the coach this way. I realized that as an introvert, my secret weapon of connection with others was curiosity and asking questions.

At Christmas, we went to the farm in Nebraska to celebrate with my family. I noticed my mom looked puffy, her legs were swollen, and she had gained weight in her abdomen area. She was sitting a lot at home and not being very active. I was worried about her health.

I had decided to follow through with "trying new things" for my new phrase. I was eager to have some new experiences.

Chapter Twenty-Seven
Trying New Things

Getting out of my comfort zone and trying new things was cued up by the success I had experienced with the hockey families. I thought I was ready to explore new things. My life was happy. I thought Tom and I were doing well. We were both working and had more money, which gave us more resources. My therapy with Ken had paid off in feeling more secure and comfortable in my own skin. I was ready to experience new things. It had become important to me to keep the boys busy as well; I saw the benefits in their lives, too.

One beautiful summer day, Tom, Jordan, Dylan, and I met with some new friends for a hike. This was a couple that had a beautiful glow about them. They invited us to go to a place in Pennsylvania called Ricketts Glen. They said it was beautiful, with lots of waterfalls. We met them because Jordan went to school with their son, and we had both had natural childbirth at home. The couple had brought a bag of organic apples and some dehydrated fruit. When they offered an apple to us, I said, "no, thank you." However, Tom and the kids took an apple and commented on the amazing flavor of the apple. The husband explained the fruit was organic, giving it higher nutrition and a wonderful flavor. They offered it to me a second time, and I was curious about it, so I said, "Yes." I took a bite of the apple, and the flavor was fresh and sweet, with a tiny tang. It filled my mouth with juice. The wife talked to me about organic food and their philosophy and beliefs. She explained they were raw foodists. I knew nothing about this way of eating or what it could mean. She was patient and kind and answered my questions during the hike. After our hike, I tried their dried fruit, and their food tasted delicious. I remembered what I had learned about fresh food and thought *this is fresh food, Janna!*

After our hike, they invited us for dinner at their house. They had a beautiful apartment above the restaurant they owned. The kitchen was designed with lots of countertop space and no oven or stovetop. A strange box with knobs and removable thin plastic shelves was on the outer edge of a counter. Hanging above it was a three-tiered basket holding loads of fruit. They told me the box was a dehydrator. They called it the Excalibur. The refrigerator had tons of organic banana stickers covering the surface. I couldn't understand a kitchen without a stove, but I wondered how they stayed healthy while eating only raw fruits and vegetables. I kept asking them if they only ate raw food, *really? I need to learn more about this.*

For dinner, the husband made a salad with freshly chopped raw beets. I had not seen beets made in this way before, and they looked and tasted delicious. I thought they came in a can. He added raw nuts and fruit. I don't remember all the ingredients or even the dressing, but it was delicious! I was becoming convinced.

These two people were two of the kindest, most vibrant people I had ever met, and they showed me a way of life I never knew existed. The way they glowed with good health and joy was attractive and inspiring. I wanted to try this raw thing as a part of my yearly commitment.

During the summer, I went to the family farm with my boys, I noticed my mom was eating more organic. She had been struggling with weight gain, inflammation, and some of her own health issues. She had gone to a naturopath in the city and had added vitamins and supplements to her diet. She was eating differently. More fruits, nuts, seeds, and vegetables. The naturopath had recommended eating six small meals a day, with no meat, and increasing organic vegetables and fruit, unsalted seeds, and nuts. They used the term whole foods. She told me they had her eat organic fruit with nuts between meals to help her blood sugar stabilize. I began doing this with her.

During our stay on the farm I discovered organic produce was hard to find. We would buy it when it was available. However, Mom and I would often drive three hours to get quality organic whole foods. The nuts were raw, with nothing added to them. We ate apples with almonds, blueberries with cashews, and black cherries with pecans. I remember thinking how much healthier my mom looked. We talked about how worried I was for her at Christmas.

I felt frustrated with this farming community's disparaging organic plant-based food supply and consciousness. I was struggling to understand how I had better access to organic fruit and vegetables in my small city community than they had in a farm town.

I stopped eating red meat altogether, and I decreased the amount of all the other meats I was eating. I felt better than I had in years when I started eating this way. I didn't realize it then, but the increase in fruits and nuts was a step toward my new way of eating.

The first time we drove by the feed lots on our way to get groceries, I had this thought: *Look at how gross that place is. Those cows are standing in their own feces, all packed together. It smells disgusting and it can't be good for the planet. I feel sick looking at it. Gosh, if no one ate red meat, it could be an organic apple orchard or something cool like that.*

When I was back home in Pennsylvania, I found a store that sold raw, unsalted nuts and organic fruit. I tried to plan my day to eat six smaller meals.

Then I learned about The China Study. This book describes the science from a study done in China. The study validated that a whole food plant-based (vegan) diet could reverse or cure some severe diseases. It mentioned high blood pressure, diabetes, cancer, and heart disease. Tom had high blood pressure. When he was twenty-six, he had surgery to repair a Patent Ductus Arteriosus. A valve at the bottom of a person's heart. It is intended to close when a baby is born. His mom and dad had diabetes. I had cancer and heart disease in my family genetics, and I was curious about the compelling claim of improved health. I was already concerned about all the genetics my children would be inheriting, and I had seen how eating helped my mother's health.

In June of 2007, I found out Tom started drinking again. We had been married for 11 years. During the next ten years, he had times of sobriety, but it was inconsistent. I feared for his life. He had gone to NJ to help his parents remodel their main bathroom. When Jordan's birthday came and went, and he had broken promises to be there and stopped answering his phone. I knew he was drinking. I knew sober Tom would never miss his son's birthday. Drug addict alcoholic Tommy couldn't get himself there. Life at home as a mom and business owner continued in spite of Tommy's relapse. I imagined there would be difficult times ahead. I would protect my children the best I was able. *I am grateful for all the tools I have.*

I became more curious and excited about the farmers' markets after my experience with the lack of organic produce in Nebraska. Markets gave small human food farmers a place to sell what they grew. One farmer sold organic and non-GMO fruits and vegetables. I had to arrive early, or she would sell out of her fair in the first couple of hours. Year after year, I watched her provide more fruits and vegetables while selling out more quickly. She was a hardworking, local farmer providing certified organic produce to our community. When the other farmers at the market and the consumers saw she was always busy and selling out, the result was more of them became organic and non-GMO. That is what I call attraction rather than promotion.

The Pennsylvania farmer's market was the first place I saw brussel sprouts on the vine they grew on. The farmer had cut them at the base of the thick woody stem, and when I bought them, they had to be removed from the stem. They were the most delicious fresh brussel sprouts I have ever eaten. They were not certified organic, but they were local, grown without pesticides or the use of fossil fuels to get them to the market. They were delicious.

I learned about the idea of a container garden from a woman at the farmer's market. I met a beekeeper, and he told me about beekeeping. I met a potter and took a class on making cups, bowls, and plates. I met the local people growing my food. This experience nurtured my body, mind, and spirit. It was a joyful connection. Trying new things opened a whole new world of health and possibility in my life and the lives of my family.

Chapter Twenty-Eight
Congruency

The definition of congruency for me is when my thinking, feeling, and behavior are aligned. My mom said, "I love you," but she didn't hug me. I didn't benefit from knowing what she was thinking, but in my mind, the two were not congruent. As a child, I grew up with so much incongruence in my life that I constantly felt confused and distressed. My father said he loved me, but I didn't have any face-to-face or phone contact with him for months at a time.

Congruency is a beautiful way to evaluate if my behavior is healthy, if a relationship is healthy, or if an organization is healthy. Congruency helps me to get clarity when I feel confused. It helps me in relationships because if a person tells me we are friends, but they don't spend time with me, I know we aren't friends we are acquaintances.

Tommy was still drinking sometimes and sober at different intervals. I was clear that I couldn't trust what he said. I never really knew if he was sober or not. I took on all the responsibility for our children. I took the boys to all their hockey practices and games. I was contracted with the school district and I aligned my work schedule with their school days. I drove them to school and picked them up. I helped them with their homework, and I put them to bed at night. I worked harder in therapy to fix myself because I knew I was powerless over Tom. *I am broken. If I was a mentally healthy, stable person, then this would not be happening to me. I must be doing something wrong for life to be so hard and unfair.*

I tried to say "yes" more when Tom wanted to spend money on toys and things I didn't value. I tried to control his sobriety with manipulation and punishment. I hoped if he was happier then he would get clean and sober again. I knew I wasn't ready to be a single mother with one income. I came up with a plan I thought was a solution. *I will stay with him and build my own life without discussing it with him.* I got sick, too.

My control and perfectionism seemed to rescue my sick mind. I stayed overly busy and used movies, television, and projects to keep my mind from noticing what was happening around me. Hypervigilance is a gift and a curse. It kept me from feeling, and it gave me the energy to change. I had learned not to focus on others, so change had to be within me.

I bought *The China Study* on Audible. I had looked it up and could see the print copy was a substantial, thick, scientific book. I purchased the audiobook in an abridged format. I was intimidated by the science and the number of pages in the text. However, I still wanted the information. *The China Study*, written by T. Collin Campbell, Ph.D., and Thomas M. Campbell M.D. was direct, engaging, fact-filled, and convincing. It's rare for me to read non-fiction without an argument in my mind. This book left me without any dispute. I wanted to rid my diet of anything from an animal. I also was convinced I needed to eat whole foods plant-based.

On January 3, 2008, I began my journey of becoming a vegan. It has been one of the best decisions for my health and emotional healing. It has connected me in a more profound way to the earth; it promotes respect for all living creatures, and I eat like a queen. I am more truly myself in all ways. I began a life of congruency and connection.

Again, congruency for me is defined as thinking, feeling, and acting in alignment. The action of not ingesting animals improved my clarity of thoughts and feelings. I acquired freedom in knowing. I'm responsible for my health. I was taking action toward helping to heal the planet, and not harming animals. The journey of becoming vegan brought years of an incongruent life into instant alignment.

When I decided to be vegan, I didn't know I would experience the power of my decision so profoundly. It took time, energy, and action to feel the full force within my soul. Becoming vegan was not only about my health. It altered my mind, body, spirit, and the planet. *I believe it is vital for us to look at our way of farming, eating, and living on the Earth. We must be the change to help heal the Earth. I love and want to protect animals, so I do not eat anything from animals. My thinking is to protect animals from harm. My feeling is love. My behavior is, don't eat anything that harms an animal.*

For me, the change in my feelings and emotional life was impactful. I began to experience clarity with what I was feeling, and my feelings became more positive. I began to wake up more joyful. I experienced happiness in moments of my day, and when a negative thought entered my mind, I was better able to counter it with positive thinking.

I also began to understand my destructive traits better and felt a stronger connection with my positive traits. My marriage had always been a struggle, but I could see where my lack of trust and need to control was affecting our relationship. As my values came into focus, my feelings did too. They seemed to be directly linked. Congruency is the thread that connects them.

When my actions changed, I stopped eating animals, and my thoughts and feelings aligned with my actions.

My family all tried to support me the best they could. Tom and I had one more contradiction between us. It was stressful for me to share a home with a man who didn't share my new values.

"Tom, can you meet me downtown after work so we can go for a walk?" I asked him one morning.

"Um, sure."

"Okay, meet me at Wegmans at 3:00." I wanted to tell him why I'd no longer be eating animal products.

We went for a walk downtown. "Tom, I know this is the right thing for me to do. I think I'd be happier with a man who doesn't eat meat, too." I paused.

"What are you saying?"

"I'm saying I'm ready to make big changes in our marriage and I'll accept it if you're not interested in being vegetarian or vegan. I'm unsure if our marriage can sustain my new values."

"Are you going to cook all of the meals?" He asked.

"I'll continue preparing vegan food for us all. Yes."

"Okay, I will eat what you guys eat." He said.

Thankfully, I knew this was my decision, and I couldn't impose it on my family. I had been honest with Tom about my goal to share my life with a man who was vegan/vegetarian. Tom tried to be supportive of my decision. Tom and the boys ate vegetarian for about six months. It was hard for my kids when they attended a birthday party, and the only pizza there was pepperoni. Then a babysitter, who was cooler than mom, took them to Subway and bought them a sandwich with meat. They wanted his approval, so they ate meat. I hope I didn't shame them or try to control their decision during this time. I know my intention was to follow my inner values without shaming others for theirs. My goal was to approach our differences with acceptance.

I felt disappointed in the world's narrow understanding of my choice and the pressures my family experienced, but I knew I had to accept it. This was evidence of my improved mental state. I didn't control their decision, and it was a huge step in congruency with my love for them. My goal was to approach our differences with acceptance and love.

Challenging myths, thoughts, and ideas in my mind was an essential part of my healing and growth. I knew I had to challenge old beliefs to remain on the vegan path. My great-grandfather said, "A mind changed against its will is of the same opinion still." It is my responsibility to decide what I think and believe. I have yet to have another person change my mind without getting my will's agreement first. *We only eat some animals and not others. I wonder why I had normalized it was okay to eat a chicken but not an eagle, a cow but not a horse, a shrimp but not a mouse. It is curious.*

I remember soon after I decided to live a vegan lifestyle, I was helping my mom clean out her garage on the farm. It was a dusty, cobwebbed old building. There were many dead mice inside. I was joking with my mom, "They are like a little snack, a crunchy little chip," I said. She was thoroughly grossed out and told me to "shut up."

I have done years and years of research and stayed curious to address many of my beliefs. I have relied on trusted friends, books, the internet, movies, magazines, meditation, prayer, and support groups to find support and stay on the vegan path.

Congruency seemed like a difficult concept for me to grasp the first time I heard a friend talk about it. However, it has brought my life into balance in a way nothing else has. When I am confused, it supports my ability to navigate the confusion and brings me clarity.

Chapter Twenty-Nine
Health

In July of 2008, I was eating primarily raw plant-based meals. I enjoyed learning how to put foods together in new and creative ways. I also learned to taste food as it's made by Mother Earth. This was an important step because I had eaten processed foods for so long. I needed to reboot my taste buds. I bought a raw cookbook called *Alive in 5* by Angela Elliot. All the recipes were simple, with about five ingredients. It made making meals faster and simpler while I explored different techniques and approaches to eating raw whole-food meals.

I felt alive. I had more energy, and I saw my acne clear up, my bowel movements became more frequent, and my body shape changed. My hips and thighs slimmed down, my hair and nails were stronger and shinier, and my face had that natural glow I had recognized in the others who were vegan and vegetarian. I looked and felt healthy.

I experienced a deeper connection with nature. My moods became more stable, and I didn't feel the dramatic ups and downs I had felt in the past. I fell in love with Mother Earth and the magic of how she grows foods for us to consume. As I have mentioned before, the plants breathe out precisely what we breathe in. *I love this synchronicity.*

I didn't burn one meal during this time. It was wonderful not to have to scrub pots and pans. I began to see the connection between the food I eat and an inner connection to the Universe or my Higher Power. Much magic was revealed to me while eating and living in my spiritual values. The Universe will conspire to support our decision when we make a congruent, value-based, conscious decision. After I became vegan, I received support from the Universe in a fantastic way.

A close friend, an excellent cook, and a nurse had just become vegan. Her husband lived a sober lifestyle. She would be my first support on my sober vegan path. Then I met another friend, Nataly. She had been gluten-free, vegan, or sometimes pescatarian for a long time, and she was also a great cook. She was my age and lived right up the street from me. She had a vegetarian daughter. (Thanks Universe!) She shared her wisdom with me while we took long, fast-paced walks together. I loved our time together, walking and talking. Her mom lived a sober life, so she understood how important both sobriety and vegan values were in my life. We talked about all kinds of topics. Honey, leather, gluten, books, and anything else under the sun. It was pure Soulshine.

"Can you tell me why vegans don't eat honey?" I asked Nataly.

"Sure!" She replied enthusiastically. "When bees make honey, they are making it to use for themselves through times without pollen, like in the winter. Also, when honey is removed, it kills, injures, and harms some bees."

"Oh, I guess I didn't think about it in that way."

"Is there an ethical way to consume honey?" I wondered.

"Maybe we consume too much of it to be ethical. Plus, there's no way not to harm some bees."

"Okay, now can I ask you about leather?"

"Absolutely!" She answered.

"I thought leather was made from the left-over skins at meat factories."

"That may be true, but what about all the other kinds of leathers and skins? If people are no longer eating meat and continue to wear leather, the same animals will continue to be treated badly and killed for their skins. Right?"

"Mmm, I hadn't thought of it like that," I replied.

"Wool is all right; they don't kill or hurt the animals for it, right?" I speculated.

"Wool is not vegan; there's some evidence sheering can be traumatic for the animals. I phased out my leather and wool products slowly over time; it made sense to me. I didn't want to fill the landfill with products still useful." She explained.

Talking with another vegan person kept me going when I wanted to give up and quit. I wouldn't have been successful if I hadn't found like-minded people for both my sober and vegan life. To have people who understood both was pure gold. Nataly wasn't judgmental or critical in any way. She answered my many questions and thoughts with patience, love, and respect. I don't know if I would have been successful without her support.

Nataly was also talented at preparing food and showed me what it meant to eat plant-based whole foods. She explained what nightshades are (potatoes, tomatoes, peppers, and eggplant) and how they can cause pain and inflammation. She educated me on the elimination diet to help identify foods causing inflammation or other potential issues. She shared recipes and how to make them. She spoke to me about feeding my family and being compassionate and understanding of others not on this path. Her vegetarian daughter watched my boys one summer. It was such necessary support while I was beginning this lifestyle change. The walking was consistent, and I learned how important exercise was for my health and mental stability.

Tom had brought home a dog called KC Jones; he had adopted the dog from the local SPCA. I didn't want him. I felt stressed from taking on full responsibility for the boys and Tommy's unknown sobriety. I imagined a dog would become my responsibility, too. I made a boundary to keep the dog; we would all sit down and read the book *A Member of the Family* by Cesar Millan out loud together. This book is a guide to a lifetime with your dog. He describes the importance of the whole family spending time with the dog and participating in "draining their energy."

I wonder if I would be happier in life if I drained my energy at certain times. Quality time sounds good, too. I had a realization that part of my anxious life was due to not knowing how important it was to drain my energy and spend quality time with the people I cherish. Learning this information changed how I interacted with my family, KC Jones, and my friends. I started asking friends and family to go for a walk with me to spend quality time together. KC often came with Nataly and me on our power walks. He became an expert on the human sober vegan while we walked together.

My mom also became part of the sober vegan journey with me. In July of 2008, she came to visit us out East. We planned to drive back to the farm together with the boys for the summer. When she arrived at our house, I was happy to see her. She commented right away that I looked good.

"Wow, Janna you look healthy. Your skin is all cleared up and your eyes look brighter, more...blue, or something. I guess not eating meat is working for you." Then she asked, "Janna, where did you learn to bake kale like this?"

I casually say, "There is this guy called Campbell; he authored a book from a study of a group of people in China. Their diets were studied for a long period of time, and they found geographical groups of them were disease-free. Campbell explains the link between what we eat and our health." I explained. "Campbell grew up on a farm in the Midwest, like you, Mom. Would you be interested in listening to it with me on the drive home?"

"I would listen to it, but there is nothing wrong with eating meat. You know how I feel about PETA Vegans. They are not healthy." She said with adamant belief. We started the audiobook called *The China Study* in Pennsylvania; by Iowa, my mom declared, "I'll never eat meat again!" Her belief had changed, and her perspective had shifted.

She continued, "I can see the pattern in my family and their health. My parents died in their 80's, my brother died at 60, my sister died at 50's. Clearly, we are going the wrong way. I'll never give up honey, leather, or wool. I am not comfortable calling myself a vegan." She thought out loud.

"Well, you could be vegetarian," I said.

"T. Collin Campbell talks about whole foods Plant-based, that is what I believe is healthy." She was exuberant about what the book was saying. We talked about the book and her new ideas as we drove through the flat, open sky and fields of crops in Nebraska.

My mom grew up eating animals the family raised. She had plucked chickens at some point in her life, and she knew where to bring an animal to have it slaughtered for meat. It was difficult for her to challenge the beliefs she held for her entire life. When she told me stories about her childhood, they were often harsh lessons learned about the farm mindset. She talked about their dog. He was not a pet. In her mind, having a dog solely for a pet without a working purpose made no sense. Dogs were intended to contribute and work. In her later years, she showed much love and affection for my dog, KC Jones, and my brothers' dogs. This is how I know deep love is contagious.

When things in my eating became too habitual or mundane, I would get a new cookbook, look on the internet for a new recipe, or join a 29-day vegan challenge. Different people have different approaches and ideas about eating and what to eat. I often learned something new about food and myself when I explored new recipes. I found sometimes I became bored. Used bookstores and flea markets often had veg books on the shelves at 75% off the cost of the new ones. I would purchase a used book and cut off the binding. Then I would put together a three-ring binder with the recipes I liked and all the notes written on the pages.

One of the struggles I had was with rare or new ingredients. I had never heard of ingredients like nutritional yeast or nori. I would go to the store with my list in hand and realize I had no idea what nori was. I also didn't know where to find it. In the beginning, I would go to the regular grocery store. Then, I would have to go to the health food store to find these untraditional ingredients. Often, I would use them once in a recipe and then never again. I was frustrated with the amount of money I spent. It also used up my time and energy. I did find new things that have now become staples in my kitchen. I love nutritional yeast, and I use it in lots of food. Popcorn, tofu scramble, and mac and cheese are my favorites. It makes a wonderful tofu scramble. I also now keep miso around and use it in several soups and sauces.

The best resource for me was to ask other vegans about rare or unfamiliar ingredients. If they had experience I would then ask for information. Other resources I found were going to veg fests, joining cooking classes, and participating in vegan meetups where everyone brought a dish to share with the recipe.

I liked going to local restaurants and ordering foods I may not typically make at home. This last one could be tricky if I didn't like what I ordered, but if I went with my kids, we ordered family style, and we would get one or two options we knew we all liked and one to test out. Then it wasn't bad if we didn't enjoy one of the dishes.

I enjoyed searching YouTube videos with the word tutorial added to my topic. For example, "tutorial nori." Then, I would get the how-to information about cooking with nori. It's a straightforward, efficient way to gather information about anything I wanted to learn.

One of the joys of becoming vegan for me has been the taste tests. I started doing these with my kids to encourage curiosity about unfamiliar food. The market constantly adds new things. There were so many companies coming up with new kinds of milk. The same old rice and soy milk were getting a run for their money. Almond, coconut, and oat milk were entering the market. It was fun and exciting for us to try all the different kinds. After the taste test was complete with opinions heard, I would add chocolate syrup (not vegan), and the kids would drink any of them, so there was no waste. Win-win.

I enjoyed going to veg festivals, veg travel, meetups, and veg restaurants. I liked to order vegan magazines and watch veg documentaries. I felt belonging when I was in these places or reading or watching the media. It connected me to the lifestyle and my values. For me, it was about more than food. It was about my connection with myself, life, and the earth.

My mom took me to my first veg fest in the East; I was delighted about all the new vegan products to sample. I could taste test to my heart's desire! Often, the companies would give out coupons, too. We took a map of the display booth name and locations to keep notes about which products we wanted to research and explore more, buy, and not buy. It was fun and didn't require the huge financial commitment and potential waste that buying these items at the store would have cost.

I have had a love-hate relationship with exercise. When I was around five years old, I took ice skating lessons and swimming lessons. My dad wanted me to ice skate, and my mom wanted me to know how to swim. I enjoyed gym class, and I played basketball in elementary school. I also enjoyed running sprints and relay races during my grade school's Outdoor Days.

My parents didn't exercise, nor did they think it was important. After my parents divorced, my most consistent exercise was cleaning the house, doing laundry, and walking to events. I tried to participate in a dance class with a friend, but I was uncoordinated and awkward. When it was my mother's turn to pick us up from middle school, she was a no-show. I felt humiliated and decided I wouldn't participate in any organized sports. *If I would have stayed in organized sports, would I have made a choice not to do drugs and drink? I will never know.*

I was happy both Jordan and Dylan were athletic like Tom. It took time and resources to keep the boys moving, but we worked hard to be active together as a family. Tom bought the boys KTM's, and we invested in snowboards for them. Now they had hockey, too. They preferred to do sports and activities rather than stay inside and play video games.

In the second year of hockey, they both had to try out for the team they played for the prior year. Most of the kids were Jordan's age and size. Dylan was a small eight-year-old and didn't make the cut. It was a hard blow for him to be told he couldn't be on the team.

Dylan did get on a team of his peers, but it was a very small team without the benefit of much organization. Tom was coaching Jordan's team, so Dylan continued to practice with his brother's team. His team wasn't meeting his needs, and as his mother, I was very unsatisfied with a wasted year of our resources. I started doing research. I found another hockey association that was about 70 miles away. I was familiar with this town and decided to bring the boys to this arena for practices and games in the following year. The downside was the distance to our home arena and the away games were up to four hours from our home. I knew it would be a much harder season for me, but I felt the investment in their experiences was worth it. Dylan deserved a team of his own. The next season would be very different.

While I was shopping for food for our family I preferred the farmer's markets, but grocery stores were essential too. I used grocery stores to study labels, meet other like-minded people in my community and learn about products. I was trying to educate myself about what was in our food, so I would go to our local grocery store and stand in the organic/health food section for hours, reading labels and learning about the symbols. I was lucky they had created a natural food section. I was not searching through the entire store to find these products. It allowed me the time to read lots of labels.

When I saw ingredients or symbols that were unfamiliar, I would use my phone to search for them or take a picture and search later for what they meant. It was an education, for sure. I remember when I became comfortable with products that a store had; I would sometimes intentionally reach out to a different store. If I needed something specific and couldn't find it, I would grab an employee and ask for their help. Then I explored and found different foods from my regularly attended store.

It helped me stay interested in maintaining my gluten-free (GF) vegan eating without becoming too bored. The downside to finding new foods at a new store was multiple store visits in the future if I wanted the newly found food. The upside was sometimes the town or city I was visiting for a hockey game or tournament had the new item and it saved my valuable time when we traveled for hockey.

I think one of the best experiences for me was finding a locally-owned vegan grocery store. I enjoyed meeting the fabulous owners of these small businesses. The people who work at these specialty stores were usually highly knowledgeable and helpful, with a kind smile and gentle spirit. They were a great resource about the community and other places of interest for vegans too.

Focusing on exercise and health empowered me to be creative with this new way of eating and to think more about activities that I would like to increase or explore for myself. I thought I might try to learn to run in the future, I wanted to increase how much hiking I did, and I thought yoga could be interesting too. I took responsibility for my health by staying vegetarian and decided to commit to continued learning and improving what I ate. *I am proud of the progress I made, and I will continue to grow. Who knows, maybe I will have a job helping others become sober and vegan someday.* I thought cheerfully.

Chapter Thirty
Dreams

Dreams happen both while we are asleep and while we are awake. I was more focused on the awake version of dreams, but I have always had a strong connection with my world of dreams while asleep, too.

One day, I was driving around some back roads, and I saw a for sale sign for a saltbox house on a tree-covered hill. When I arrived home, I looked it up on the local real estate listing. This house checked all the boxes. It had four bedrooms upstairs and an office on the main level. It was in the woods outside of town and it came with five acres of trees, wildlife, and potential. I couldn't see or hear any of the neighbors. The build was incomplete, and we could add our own personal touches. The railings for all the steps were missing, the floors were subfloors, and the two top rooms were unfinished. The kitchen had a stone-covered wall, and there was an outside door next to the wall.

The door led to a concrete floor that could have walls and windows on all three sides, like a greenhouse. I loved having a space with three exterior sides. I imagined a greenhouse to grow my vegetables year-round in the unfinished space. *I want this house.* My dream of a vegan kitchen, husband, two kids, and a dog would be complete. The five acres gave me hours and hours of dreaming. *I can finally be happy.* I thought.

When I showed Tom the listing, he was interested in buying it too. We set up a tour of the house. While walking through the kitchen, I saw a heart-shaped rock on the stone feature. In the basement stairway was the name DYLAN, written in chalk on the concrete block wall. Serendipitous. *Dylan would love all the space, trees, and wildlife up here.* I knew we would buy this house.

We bought the house and started the remodeling process. It was a lot to handle. We were carrying two mortgages and buying supplies to do the work. Also, the boys were now playing hockey for the team that was an hour to an hour and a half away. I was driving there for hockey games and practices two to four times a week.

I was in control of the hockey, school, and work schedules for the boys and me. When I had a break and during the off-season, I would help with the remodeling. Tom focused on his work and having a good time. I had no interest in the good times. I became intense, controlling, and bossy. I wanted my dreams, so I would work hard to get them.

One evening, Tom and I were sitting on our bed talking and we disagreed about a big purchase. Tom wanted to spend money on new motorcycles, and I wanted to use the money for our remodel. He became very angry.

"Tom, money is tight right now and I think we'll need that money for flooring in the new house."

"Well, I bought this land so I could ride with the boys, and I need a motorcycle."

"Need?" I said with a sneer. "You don't need a motorcycle; we need flooring. The subfloor will get wet and dirty and be ruined if we don't install real flooring." I punctuated definitively.

Tom and I had begun to fight more often. He would make a fist and hold it in the air near my head, then growl and walk away. It was scary and intense. *I can handle this; Tommy wouldn't hit me; he's just stressed about money.*

Most weekends, the boys and I would travel to and from hockey games. When we were not at hockey games, I'd be working, cooking, and cleaning. I didn't see Tommy much. One weekend, there was an ice storm. The boy's games were canceled, and we had a weekend without any hockey. I had sent Tommy a text and received a strange response. He told me he couldn't get his new quad running to clear the road at the new house, so he was going to stay there. *I wonder if he's using again. Janna, all the signs are there. He's not texting you in his normal pattern, he's not coming home, and he has been increasingly violent with you. He's using,* my wiser self-thought. My denial was always ready with the next response. *You have no proof.*

When the storm was over, I took the day off work. I dropped off the boys at school and I drove up to the new house. There was proof. Tommy was using drugs and drinking alcohol again. I called two sober men we knew. One of them was a neighbor and knew Tommy very well. The other knew him pretty well and he worked at a treatment center. They met Tommy and me at our house in town and they took him to treatment. Tommy didn't want to go, but they handled it and convinced him he needed to go.

He was in treatment for 30 days. I kept busy with the kids, the household responsibilities, work, and my life. I was a married, single parent for 30 days.

After Tommy left, I sat down at the kitchen table and told the boys.

"Your dad is sick again," I explained. "He's been putting alcohol and drugs into his body, and it's hurting his ability to act like he normally does with us. Our friends are taking him to a place where he will be safe, and he will get help."

Then, I let them ask me questions. I know they asked me some questions, but I don't remember the details. I wanted them to know their dad was safe and they could count on me. I hoped this could be an experience we would have without trauma.

"I'm here for you both; if you need anything, I promise to take care of you," I reassured them.

I was proud of the way I handled the whole situation, but I also felt a deep sadness. It seemed like my heart was pounding softer and slower than its normal pace.

Each time I try to dream, it doesn't work out. Why is life always knocking me down? I knew there was more growing ahead, I thought perhaps honing my instincts would help.

"My fear of abandonment is exceeded only by my terror of intimacy."

— **Ethlie Ann Vare**

Chapter Thirty-One
Instincts

The definition of instincts, according to the Oxford English Dictionary, is a natural or intuitive way of acting or thinking. *My natural way of thinking is based on survival and is fight or flight. That may be, but you are changing your mind and habits; you're building in an automatic pause so you are able to choose a new path. Do this enough, and it will become a habit. When you meditate, listen for the answers; they will come.*

Tommy and I stayed married after he finished treatment and we continued to remodel the house. It went much more slowly because he was using some of his time to meet with mentors and sober friends. I was trying to stay out of his way and take care of our boys. When we moved into the house, things became tense and scary fast.

One crisp fall morning, I was getting ready to take the kids to school and go to work. Tommy was attempting to goad me into an argument. I was trying to avoid him and not respond to his aggressive dialogue. This had worked in the past when he was worked up about something. *Just keep quiet and get the hell out of here. No eye contact, get your keys, call the kids. Hurry!*

I rushed the kids out to the car and left without a word to Tommy. Then he came running out the patio door and ripped my car door open. He stood between me and the door. He started screaming at me and calling me names in front of our children. My heart was pounding in my chest and ears. My head started to buzz. *I can't let him do this in front of our children; I must get them out of here.*

"Why are you acting like such a fucking bitch!" he screamed.

"Tommy, please stop; I need to get our kids to school," I said loudly.

"I do not give a fuck about school; they need to know what a bitch their mother is; that's what they need to learn today."

I saw I had about two feet between my bumper and the steps to the deck. I put the car in drive and moved forward, causing Tommy to fall. He was safely out of the way. Then I quickly closed the door and hit the lock. Tommy was still screaming at me, but I was able to pull out of the driveway and I could leave. I took the kids to school and went to work.

Did that really happen? He must be using drugs again to act like that. He'll be better when he has time to cool down. God, I hope this doesn't mess up the boys. I never wanted this for them. This is stressful. I must maintain my health and keep a normal, sober environment for them. I can't be a single mom. Is this really better than being a single mom? I don't know.

He texted me and apologized a few hours later. I asked him to get help and apologize to the boys. He didn't do either.

The boys played hockey on two different teams, and we were on the road a lot. I spent Fridays getting food ready for the weekend travel and then traveling all weekend for home and away games.

It became challenging to juggle work, hockey, food, and household chores. I had the idea if I added eggs back into my diet, I would be able to eat the beautiful omelets made to order at the hotel where we stayed for the away games. My thought was *it's just eggs. It can't hurt me that much.* In addition to my inner thoughts, I had seen a naturopath who told me I *should* add eggs back into my diet. I knew I could find them on menus easily, and it would be more convenient.

During our away games, the parents were having potluck-style meals together. I felt different from the other parents for many reasons. I was new to the team, the only parent attending without my spouse, and I ate differently. I wanted to fit in with the group. I started eating eggs again.

I caught a cold at the end of January, and I couldn't seem to recover. Then, by early February, I had a double ear infection with both eardrums broken and because of the puss and fluid in my ears, I couldn't hear. I was also experiencing hot flashes and night sweats. Emotionally I felt sad, isolated, and frustrated.

I stopped eating eggs and started making my healing juice cocktail. This consisted of juicing carrots, apples, beets, ginger, and lime. I was drinking my healing tonic daily for two weeks. With eardrops from my PA and my tonic, I felt better in a few days.

My belief that eggs were harmless was inaccurate. When eating out and ordering gluten-free bread, I was often told it wasn't vegan; it contained eggs. I was still choosing the GF non-vegan bread. I knew I'd be sick from gluten within 24 hours. I managed how much bread I consumed, and I didn't get sick from it. I hoped someday I'd find delicious gluten-free, vegan bread.

My mom called me one morning. "Janna, I found a vegan cruise."

"Mom, that sounds great."

"T. Collin Campbell and Neil Barnard are speakers on the cruise. I would love to meet Campbell! Will Tommy watch the boys so you can come with me?"

"Um, I'll need to talk to Tom; when is it?"

"March,"

"Okay, let me talk to Tom; I'll let you know."

Tommy agreed, and we asked his parents to come up and help out with the kids.

The cruise was initially intended for people from a macrobiotic lifestyle. I learned so much about the macro lifestyle. The philosophy doesn't use much seasoning, and they believe if food is cooked, it is less work for the body to assimilate and access the nutrients. They even cook fruit, which I don't love. I came from the world of raw food where the belief is if you cook foods hotter than 110-115 degrees, nutrients are damaged, the opposite of macro.

One of the best parts of the cruise for me was meeting Neal Barnard, T Collin Campbell, and Dr. Esselstyn were the prominent presenters on the cruise. I called them "The Bigs" because they were prominent teachers of the whole food plant-based eating. On the cruise, they presented their current research and work. I saw other wonderful speakers, too.

Spending this time with my mom, learning about food and traveling was joyful. I healed my body and my relationship with my mom. It was a wonderful adventure. The food was okay, but not great. I'm definitely more of a raw food person.

In March of 2011, I returned home from the cruise and had a day off to get settled back home again. I took the kids to school and returned home. Tommy had been angry about the vegan cruise. I didn't understand why. He accused me of cheating on him and I responded with sarcastic humor. "I tried, but no one would have me," I said with a laugh. I was standing in the laundry area in our main bedroom closet.

"You need to remember we live in the trees. No one around us can hear anything." He responded with a cold, calm threat.

I felt goosebumps on my body, and a cold chill ran up and down my spine. I stopped sorting laundry, and I casually went into Dylan's room and closed the door. Then I turned the lock. *Shit, where is my phone?* I stayed there with the door locked until I saw Tommy get into his truck and leave. Then I picked up the cordless phone and I called my therapist, Ken.

I relayed the phrase to Ken.

"I take death threats very seriously," Ken said.

"I'm not sure what to do," I said. *Ken called it a death threat?* I thought. *Did he threaten to kill me?* I was having a hard time feeling any emotions. My mind was in the dream again, just like walking in the hall at school in 1991, but I was isolated and *very* alone this time.

"Janna, do you have a piece of paper?" Ken got my attention.

"Yes," I replied as I walked quickly down the steps to my office. Ken gave me a number for the women's shelter. I called them as soon as I hung up and made an appointment for an hour later.

While I was driving, I started to make a plan.

This is the end of my marriage. I don't trust that I'm safe with him. He must be using again; I cannot leave him; he might overdose. I have to get myself together and leave him for my own safety. What if I misinterpreted what he meant? How did I let myself become so dependent and alone? I need to call my mom, I need help.

I met with a woman from the local abuse shelter. She encouraged me to file a protection from abuse order with the courts. I didn't trust the system and was uncomfortable going to court to get a protection order. It was just a piece of paper.

162

I'd interpreted for some presenters that talked about the cycle of abuse and they said the most dangerous time for an abused person was when they tried to leave. I believed them. *He could kill me faster than the police could be at our home.* I finally started to feel afraid.

"Mom?" My voice cracked.

"What's wrong?" She said. *I just want to be with my family now.* I began to cry. "Tommy threatened me, I think." I had called him Tommy when he was behaving childishly. My mom knew that was my pattern before I did.

"Tell me everything; we'll make a plan. I'm getting on the first plane out of here."

Thank God she is such a force. I thought.

"You want me to come, right?" She asked.

YES! "I do, but let me make it through tonight; the boys have hockey, and we'll be busy this weekend. I'll always keep my phone with me. I'll call you before I go to sleep and when I wake up in the morning. When Tommy leaves in the morning, I'll call, and we can come up with the next steps."

"I'm afraid for you, Janna." She said.

I couldn't safely leave the marriage right away, and my family was deeply concerned for me. They all supported me in special ways. My dad and brothers called and gave me advice. Some of it was helpful, and some of it was attempted support from people who were afraid for their loved one, me.

I told my mom, "If I leave, he will chase me and that seems dangerous. If the boys are with me, I don't think he will do anything. After I drop them off, I will go to work. I will pick them up and we will stay together."

My routine would be my security and control. I trusted our separateness to be my safety net. I wanted stability for the boys for as long as I could maintain it. I knew all hell would break loose soon.

Tom and I had been living two separate lives for about three years. I went to bed and rose early. He went to bed late and slept late. We passed each other occasionally or saw each other at the occasional hockey game. There was limited interaction between us.

For most of that first night I laid in bed, unable to drift off. I listened for Tommy's truck coming up the dirt road. When he finally came home, it was very late and I pretended to be asleep. He went into the basement and then left the house again. I felt relieved. *There will be no confrontation tonight.*

I called my mom. "Hello?"

"Mom, he came home, rooted around in the basement, and left again."

"Okay, are you able to sleep?" She asked.

"I'll try," I said. "Good night, Mom."

"Please call me if anything changes. If not, let's talk in the morning."

When I felt afraid Tom would hurt me, I lived in a prison. Fear was the gatekeeper. It was exhausting and didn't allow me to feel other hope-based feelings. I had the thought *fear could permeate my life like cancer if I'm not connected to my Higher Power.*

While I was consumed by fear, I was spiritually sick. I wasn't trusting my Higher Power to guide my life. I didn't trust myself. I was addicted to control in place of inner security and attachment with my authentic self. My inner thoughts were so negative and critical, which led to self-judgment without grace, and rejecting love from others. *My boundaries are not keeping me safe or happy. Why?* I asked myself. Then it came to me. *Boundaries are another path of control, Janna. Try structure instead.*

My mind saw a picture of scaffolding on the side of a building that could be removed and rebuilt over and over. It was strong yet flexible. The boundary wall began to crumble. Creating structure for myself was the way I learned to slowly let go of control. Then, I began to learn to trust myself.

What does a successful structure look like in your life? If I know I'm going to a restaurant, I can call ahead to let them know how I eat, look up the menu online, and get an idea about what I will order. Then, I can decide if I want to go to the restaurant. How are structure and boundaries different?

I looked up the definition for structure: to construct or arrange according to a plan; give pattern or organization to. *A plan is like a map.* I thought. *I can take many paths to end up in a chosen location. It's flexible; I know the end result, but I'm able to navigate through my choices. As I learned the routes of the roads better, I'd be able to arrive at the destination by the route with the least difficulty.*

Boundaries are a loving and respectful way for me to let others know my beliefs. I don't eat anything from an animal is my boundary, I reasoned. *When I eat gluten-free bread that contains eggs, I'm in structure. My thinking is grey, not black and white. Structure is the grey area that flexes within the boundaries.*

As she had promised, my mom came to stay with me. Tommy was not happy when she arrived. I didn't prepare him for her visit.

He arrived home late one night, and she was there. She brought her blow-up mattress and put it on the floor in the same room where I slept. I made another bed in a separate room for Tom to use. I moved all his belongings to the basement with his tools. She stayed with me to make sure I would remain safe.

Tom stopped coming home regularly. He came home a couple of times and asked me for money. I said "no."

Thank God she was such a force. When she and I were together, I knew I was safe. She helped me navigate the courts, find an incredible lawyer, and take care of Jordan and Dylan. She did most of the cooking of healthy vegan meals. I received a few long and meaningful hugs. I was grateful she was there with me. Without my mom's support, I may not have gotten out alive. I'll never know if Tom would have hurt me.

I confirmed during this time that Tom was using drugs again. I found a prescription with his name for suboxone from a doctor outside of our town.

I felt sad, afraid, alone, and lonely. I was also depressed. I was making an effort to stay connected to my feelings as they came up, which was a new experience. It required pauses and breathing to think about how I was feeling and not deny it or stuff it down.

I pulled out the picture of the faces with the feeling words and took a picture of it on my phone. Several times a day, I would look at the picture and think about what I was feeling, the color and shape, and the location. I wanted to process this event in real time.

Throughout the divorce, I felt depressed. I was not yet healthy enough to handle all the deeper feelings as they came up, but I was trying to stay connected to myself. I struggled to make decisions. I wanted to be alone in my car. I sighed many times throughout the day. I became more controlling, independent, and black-and-white with my thinking. My children seemed to prefer their addicted father to their controlling mother.

My divorce was expensive and brutal. Watching Tom in his addiction was devastating. Before we separated, Tom urinated on my clothes, jumped on my computer laptop, and burned all my tax records while I was at work and my mom was with her quilting group. I filed a police report, however, I still didn't request a protection from abuse when it was suggested. I believed Tom was sick and that jail was no place for a person with an addiction.

I learned more about myself during this year. My instincts while I was in trauma were survival traits. I was born with the instinct to eat when I feel hungry, sleep when I feel tired and fight or run when I feel afraid. I developed the instinct to ignore my needs and take care of my children first. I also learned to rely on myself, even though I didn't trust myself. Yet. I realized my instincts were damaged, similar to my beliefs.

Growing up in a dysfunctional home influenced my thoughts and behaviors, which fueled my instincts. I became focused on the path of survival. I was wired for a life of trauma and stress. It paid me in adrenaline, cortisol, and norepinephrine highs. My inner need for danger led to feelings of excitement and anger. My inner warrior wanted to be fierce. I was sick and had not yet found a solution to my control addiction.

If I'm going to change my instincts and learn to let go of control, I want to work on my intuitive thoughts. The roots of the tree. I need to ask my Higher Power for help.

Chapter Thirty-Two
Intuitive Thoughts

I pulled out my phone and read: "Intuitive thought is going with one's first instinct and reaching decisions quickly based on automatic cognitive processes." *This is going to take a lot of time and practice.*

I had a Buddhist friend, and she taught me to chant. Chanting helped me get out of the feelings and have a break from my hurt inner dialogue. The chanting kept me busy in a positive way. *Namu Myoho Renge Kyo.* To my ears, it sounded like *nom yo ho Renge Keyo.* It's Sanskrit, meaning to devote or dedicate oneself. It's a vow to embrace my Buddha nature. It's a commitment not to surrender to my difficulties but to prevail over suffering.

I would only sleep a few hours each night. Chanting was the only way I could calm my mind and get back to sleep. Some nights, I would chant, cry, chant, cry. I was grateful for the chanting and the crying. I increased my prayer and meditation. I started praying on my knees each time after making my bed and before getting into my bed at night. I would often stay on my knees in silence with my hands crossed together and resting in front of me.

One morning in February before work, I had finished praying and was just on my knees with my hands folded, leaning on my bed. I heard *file the request to move back to Colorado today.* I heard it clearly. I had an intuitive thought. *Trust yourself.*

On my way to work, I called my lawyer, "I need to get permission to move home to Colorado today!"

She was quiet, and then she said, "Janna, no woman in this county has ever obtained permission to leave with their kids."

I said, "Okay, but promise me you will do it today."

At my behest, she agreed.

My mom returned to Colorado briefly to take care of some things. While she was back in the West, she put together a book of statistics about how the community in Colorado was safer and more equipped to support me as a single mother. She included information about hockey arenas, skate parks, and family support. She also had information about the schools, the survey statistics, and government programs to help single parents. Most importantly, when she came back to Colorado, she and my brother rented a home where we could land if we were given permission to move. She drew from her experience as a single parent and included all the compelling information my lawyer would need to make the winning argument. The book was a three-ring binder full of my mom's brilliant research. My lawyer was impressed.

My mom returned and we developed a routine. She joined a quilting group and I worked. We would take care of the boys together and on the brutal days when Tommy had them, Mom planned all kinds of outings and events to help me stay busy and keep my mind off my aching heart.

Occasionally, we'd return home, and things would be out of place. One day, I found grass clippings in my bed; another day, I found a drawer on a side table open. I didn't find anything noticeable missing. I imagined Tom was coming to the house and being in a familiar clean, safe space. I never found him there when I arrived home. Each time I found evidence of his presence, I paused. *I pray for your protection and sobriety; I know you are suffering.*

The life of an addict is miserable and filled with hopelessness and despair. Divorce is, too. I imagined he came on the days he wanted some comfort and rest from the addicted life he was living. Strangely, I didn't feel afraid. I felt my own despair at watching his addiction, and I chose compassion for him over fear.

One weekend when Tom had the boys, we drove to the Animal Farm Sanctuary in Woodstock and stayed at the Bed & Breakfast. There was a turkey that followed me around and kept putting his head on my leg. It kind of freaked me out, but it was endearing at the same time. I started calling him Tom, Tom the turkey.

I was told by a mutual friend that Tom was living in a house he was planning to flip. They told me the name of the street and the area where it was. I wasn't familiar with the street.

Then, I received a call from the fire department about a month later. "Hello?"

"Is this Janna?"

"Yes."

"This is Fire Marshal Smith. I'm here with your children; they are alone, and there was a fire at their dad's house."

"Oh my god, I'm on my way!" I hung up the phone and told my mom,

"We have to go to Tommy's house now! There was a fire."

"Janna, did you get the address?"

"Shit! No! Come on, I'll find it!" I drove to the street where I knew the school bus picked up my boys when they stayed with Tom, and then I took a deep breath and prayed. *God, please help me know where to go; my children need me now.*

"I'm going North up this street," I told my mom. She was silent.

As we drove around the curve in the road, I saw the fire trucks. *I did it!* My intuitive thought had taken me in the right direction, and I found my kids. They were safe.

Tom had used some tung oil to treat some raw wood at his new house. He threw it in a trash can on the back porch where the sun had shone on it. The rags in the can started on fire. It remained relatively small, and no one was hurt.

The courts gave us shared custody, but my kids were blaming me, and they were angry with my boundaries and rules. Dylan had been caught with marijuana at his middle school, and Jordan was also implicated. We cooperated fully with the police. The boys had been put on probation with community service hours. I resisted blaming Tommy but wondered if he had any involvement.

Daily prayer and meditation supported my healthy inner thoughts. I was calmer throughout the day and my mind was managing the stress. I would repeat affirmations to help me navigate the tumultuous times. *You are safe, you are healthy, you are kind. You are safe, you are healthy, you are kind. You are safe, you are healthy, you are kind.*

Several months later, when the court date for permission to move back home to Colorado came up, Tom was arrested for a drug-related charge and showed up in shackles and an orange jumper. I was given full custody of the boys and permission to go where I had family and community support. My years of sobriety, a safe place to land and Tom's history with drugs and alcohol empowered the courts to give me permission. We arranged for my boys to complete their probation and community service, then they were free to leave.

I hated the idea of separating Jordan and Dylan from their dad. I had experienced this kind of separation and knew it would be hard for them. Having family nearby for support and having a safe community with resources was the best way for me to take care of myself. Only then, could I take care of my children too. I was healing. I was beginning to trust and care about myself.

My mom loved me in the same way when she brought us to Grandpa Carl and Grandma Alice. I completely understood my mom's decision to move closer to her family after her divorce. I thought about how important an open mind and perspective are for healing. I was able to let go of the pain and loss from my move away from my own father. My Higher Power lives in these profound moments.

Chapter Thirty-Three
One Day at A Time

I can get through anything if I remain grounded in the 24-hour mindset. Starting at 24 hours gave me the energy to learn to focus on the present moment gradually.

In the early commitment to my sobriety, I remember worrying about all the potential events I would miss out on if I stayed sober: my twenty-first birthday, graduation, wedding, and traveling to vineyards in Europe. The truth was I didn't miss out on any of these momentous events. I still celebrated, and I remember each wonderful, stressful, interesting moment. Only because I was sober. I enjoyed the drink made from the grapes at the vineyard even more than I would have enjoyed the wine.

I spent a year focused on one day at a time. Each day, I greeted it with a decision to be ready to do what I could for that day and that day only. When I needed to plan a future event, I learned to plan what I could then take my mind back to the moment in the current day.

If my mind wandered into details of the past, I gently told myself, *There is no changing the past,* and I would look around me and bring my focus back to what I could see, smell, hear, and feel.

What if staying in the day will allow my mind to learn to stay in the moment? I pondered. *What happens if I focus on acceptance of the current moment? Could I let go of control with this practice?*

When I maintained mindfulness in the present moment and the practice of acceptance, I found letting go easier. I also found I didn't have the need for control.

I wanted to be present inside my body and feel connected. I learned to appreciate how my body supports life and energy. I was practicing thoughts of acceptance about my pear-shaped body, thick legs, and arms. I wanted to be free to connect with my best health. I needed to feel, hear, and see what my body was communicating so I could respond to its needs. This would later become part of learning to love me. Listening to my inner thoughts and building trust in myself required time and practice.

Listening is an engaged interaction. Listening to my mind, feeling the feelings, and being connected to the image in the mirror as a healthy body.

I knew I had lost the taste for specific foods when I listened to myself. One time, I accidentally received a latte made with cow's milk. I took a big gulp before I realized they made it with animal milk. I swallowed it, and it tasted horrible. I could taste the cow! I'm not sure if I tasted the pus, blood, or what, but it tasted so foul I thought I would throw up. Once, I tasted some white fish in a restaurant, and it did not taste good.

My sense of smell also changed. A local store had vegan meats and cheeses stocked next to the seafood. I'd have to hold my breath, run to the shelf, grab what I needed, and run away. It was an affront to my senses, so I stopped shopping there.

I knew the move and starting over in my hometown, with my family around, would have its own special kind of stress. I remained grounded in the 24-hour mindset.

I sold most of my furniture, bought and packed a pull-along trailer, and moved home to Northern Colorado.

In August of 2012, we once again made the long drive from Pennsylvania to Colorado, with a stop at my mother's home in Nebraska. Finally, we arrived at the Colorado rental house. I was back home, and it felt great.

The healing sun, the foothills in the West, and the smiling faces of the people put me at ease. I had family around me and was starting to let go of the constant stress of surviving. Our first task was to find the hockey rink and show it to the boys. The second was the skate parks.

I didn't find a job immediately. I wanted to help the boys transition and be available for their activities. I started going to garage sales and buying cheap furniture to repair, distress paint, and sell. It was therapeutic.

I signed both boys up for hockey right away. Once again, practices, games, and school consumed us. It was amazing to sit in the stands with my family. My mom and my brother, Chad were at most games. When we traveled near other members, they would come. It was wonderful to share hockey with my whole family. I loved it. Some of my most cherished, joyful memories are of being at games and watching my boys while sitting in the middle of my whole family.

There were five skateboarding parks in the area, so Jordan and Dylan were at a skate park when we weren't busy with hockey. All the remaining time was spent on a ski slope.

I didn't request Tom give me any child support during our custody hearing before I left. I wanted to give Tom a chance to focus on getting clean and sober again, and I had received money from the sale of our two houses, so I was doing okay. He was court-ordered to pay for half of the cost of sports, medical, dental, clothing, etc. He didn't help. I ran out of money fast. I had to go back to work.

My dad decided to move back to Colorado. His health was not good, and he said the winters in North Dakota were too hard on him. He bought an old trailer home, and his brother Gary helped him get packed up and drive his two trucks to Colorado.

He mentioned to me that he would give his old green truck to Jordan. I told him I needed to think about it. I knew if Jordan had a truck, he would have to pay for repairs, insurance, and gas. I didn't trust him to take on that financial responsibility yet. I knew I couldn't afford to add any of these things to my plate. I was also concerned that if he was drinking or using and had an accident, I would be "the responsible" party. I wasn't willing to take that risk.

My dad talked to Jordan without my permission and brought the truck to my house. I imagine he thought he could manipulate me into giving in. That was not the case. I took the keys from Jordan and locked them in my safe.

Jordan didn't like the kids in Colorado, and he was starting to use drugs and alcohol again. He missed his girlfriend and his friends. He was angry with me. I imagine my control, tough love, and drug testing created a barrier in our relationship.

"Mom! Grandpa gave me the truck! It's a gift!"

"No, Jordan, you are not allowed to have the truck until you are clean and sober and can afford to pay for it." Jordan was standing in the doorway of my bedroom; he lurched forward and raised his fist at me like he would punch me in the face.

"Give me the keys!" he shouted.

I felt startled and afraid. I recognized the cycle of being afraid of men in my life. "Please leave my room. We can talk when you are calm." I said.

He left my room.

Breathe.

As I sat on my bed I thought. *This is a pattern. I'm the common thread here. My brother was violent with me often; my father was violent with me once when he was drunk, and I was thirteen. My husband was violent with me a couple of times in our seventeen-year marriage, then threatened to kill me. What am I doing to cause this pattern? I want this to change.*

I knew I had work to do. I didn't understand the why or where of this pattern, but I knew when the time was right, I'd do the work to heal. For now, I only needed to think of the moment and the 24 hours ahead.

Chapter Thirty-Four
Acceptance

The definitions of acceptance:

1. The action of consenting to receive or undertake something offered.

2. The action or process of being received as adequate or suitable, typically to be admitted into a group.

3. Agreement with belief in an idea, opinion, or explanation.

Acceptance is a brilliant practice and it seemed to be the shortcut to success with all the other words and phrases I had worked on. Acceptance is the key to unlocking all the doors.

In July of 2013, I took Jordan and Dylan to the airport and loaded them on the airplane to see their dad. I missed them and was lost without them. I spent much of my time binge-watching TV shows and movies. I watched the Dexter series in two weeks.

"Hi, guys! How's PA?" I asked through the phone while sitting on my orange crushed velvet secondhand couch.

"Good," Dylan said. "Fun!" Jordan said.

"How is your dad?" I asked.

"He is good, Mom," Jordan said with defensiveness.

"Good," I said. We talked about the friends they had reconnected with and the activities they were doing. As the conversation was ending, Jordan spoke up. "Mom, can I talk to you alone?"

"Sure, Jordan."

"I love you, Dylan; see ya soon, okay?"

"Okay, bye, Mom." I heard Dylan's footsteps as he walked away.

"What's up, Jordan? Is everything okay?"

"I just wanted to let you know I'm not coming back to Colorado."

"Oh," I said. *I wondered if this was going to happen.*

"I miss my friends and Kay, and I just like it better here."

"Well, let me talk to your dad and think about it."

I understood his desire to be back East. My heart knew pain and grief were coming. I tried not to feel abandoned, but it was my default nature. I also felt compassion and understanding. He had a girlfriend there and missed his friends.

I had done some sleuthing before I sent my kids to visit him, and Tom was telling me he was sober. My friends who lived there reported seeing him and believed he was telling me the truth. After I talked to Tom and some of my friends from the area, I was ready to surrender and accept Jordan's decision. I believed my community would support Jordan if he asked. I missed him every day.

I said prayers for Jordan's happiness and safety often. I would dedicate my chanting to him. A day never went by when I didn't think of him and hope for his highest and best life. I felt a pain in my heart when I thought about not seeing him, so I tried not to think about it.

Dylan seemed to adjust to the absence of his brother. He had some close friends in Colorado and spent a lot of his time with them. He continued to play hockey, skateboard, and snowboard. He seemed like he was doing well, except in school. He hated waking up early, doing homework, and taking tests. I tried to support him as much as I could. However, without an official ADD diagnosis, the school felt no need to provide him with any real support. He was finally put with a teacher he connected with and then placed into classes like art, woodworking, and also study time to help him.

I thought he was doing well until I began to see the addiction behavior. It was the same behavior I saw in Tommy and Jordan.

I must be better with Dylan than I was with Jordan. I feared for what was to come again. I prepared myself for the possibility of a long roller coaster ride.

In December 2014, my mom found out she had a lime-sized tumor in her colon. My mom had been vegan for six years, and she told me she felt betrayed by her body. She believed being whole foods plant-based (WFPB) would keep her disease-free.

"Janna," She said in the ER after the results of her scan were revealed. "Conventional medicine will only be able to remove the tumor. When the surgeon cuts into the cancerous area, cancer cells will be distributed throughout my body, through my bloodstream. I need to find a naturopathic doctor to help my body get rid of the cancer. I want to follow a non-conventional treatment."

My mom asked us to get ahold of my dad, but he was not answering his phone. I wasn't used to having my dad available physically and I found it hard to remember he was living in Colorado. I also saw him as broken and didn't trust him. I was trying to shift my thinking about my dad, but it was complicated.

She had the tumor surgically removed and spent the week of Christmas in the hospital recovering. Her children, grandkids, and family all surrounded her. They moved her to the big room at the end of the hall because of all the visitors who came to the hospital.

Dylan suggested we get a Charlie Brown tree and bring it to her room in the hospital, so we did. We also replaced the plain red Christmas ball ornament with a red Bones Brigade ornament (skateboarding company).

When she was in the hospital, I lost my faith.

I remember one night when I arrived home from a long day at work and the hospital, I needed a run. I felt angry and stressed out. I laced up my running shoes, grabbed my dog, and went out for a late-night run. It was December, but I don't remember feeling cold. I do remember I stopped running and sat on the curb.

I started screaming and crying. Then I cursed God. "Why am I suffering again? Life has been harder for me than other people. What did I do to deserve this? I hate my life. If you are so powerful, why am I struggling? Why aren't you protecting me from this misery? If you take my vegan mother before my alcoholic father, I am done with you forever!" I screamed, I threatened, and I blamed.

"You failed me again. I am done with you. I no longer accept any form of God."

God is a made-up way to control people and reward people who are rich and privileged.

Then I stood up and walked home. I felt angry with God. I blamed him for my difficulties.

After the surgery, she continued with natural treatments as a self-pay patient. Her treatment included a hyperbaric chamber, vitamin C infusions, and an organic, sugar-free, WFPB diet. The conventional doctors were impressed with her recovery.

Dylan had started smoking pot, drinking and dabbing. He also started getting into trouble. I knew what the signs were, and I wasn't in denial. When he was picked up by the police, I showed up. I showed up for court, and I cooperated within the system. I would breathe, pause, and remember to accept it. I didn't pray.

I talked to a man one day who had been going through the same thing with his daughter. He talked about the disease and how important his compassion was. He explained that when he kept his mind and his heart in compassion, he didn't criticize and blame his daughter. He talked about her battle with addiction. He used the same word I had used to describe my mother's cancer, "battle." It completely shifted my perspective. This wasn't personal: my son was fighting for his life.

I got ready to fight for his life too. My weapons were compassion, love, and tolerance. My goal was healing, support, and safety. I knew it would be a hard path, but I was going to show up for all of it.

When I remain in acceptance for each moment, I can feel the feelings, think the thoughts, and clearly respond. When action is needed, I can get busy. **These are the tools I now had to navigate life.**

Chapter Thirty-Five
Connection

I read a Brené Brown book where she talked about values. She created a list for her readers to identify core values, in which to build their best life.

While talking about the list with a co-worker, she said, "Mmm, why is connection on the list?"

"Oh, I think it's a fabulous value; I'm deeply connected to the earth and the food she provides. I'm connected with animals and people. I'm connected to my body, my feelings, and my mind. What I like about our work is the physical connection to the words and language. I could go on, but you get the idea" In my explanation to her, I realized it was my core value.

In the world of psychology, connection to myself is called attachment. According to Brené Brown connection to a group of people is called belonging.

I'm an introvert, so connecting with people is challenging, but the connection with the earth, the moment as it's unfolding, the food I put into my body, and the animals around me are all ways my energy gets restored. When I mess up a connection, it feels painful. It causes a rupture in my soul. I wonder if this rupture is what created my trauma. Trauma is a cue to my whole self that I need to learn to behave differently, fast. This must be how I survived my childhood.

In October, I was promoted at work and was trying to learn to run a million-dollar call center with a staff of eighteen. While I was at work, I received a call from the hospital across the street; my dad was experiencing issues and went to the emergency room.

I left work and drove to the ER. I could see my dad was in bad shape and was declining. The doctor confirmed for me that years of smoking and drinking had taken a toll on his health. He implied that my dad might only live a few years. He told my father he must stop smoking. My father had smoked since he was 12 years old.

My mom's rental lease was up in April, and I now had an extra room in my condo. I asked her to move in with Dylan and me. I wanted to keep an eye on her, and I knew she would be an incredible support to me. In January, my mom was told she was in remission from her cancer. *Life's getting better.*

In April 2015, my mom moved in. I was grateful to have her there. We had family over for the holidays and talked, cooked, cleaned, and ran errands together. We put puzzles together and played cards. Chad was there often, Sean visited occasionally, and I was thrilled to have my family all around me. I felt loved and cared for. A part of me knew when Tom threatened my life, it impacted my family too. Feeling afraid and powerless affects people. It brought us all together. We lived in the same state for the first time in over thirty years.

I felt the absence of Jordan intensely. I tried to include him with phone calls when we were gathered. Unfortunately, there wasn't as much communication as I wanted between us.

One day, when I arrived home from work. I told my mom I planned to make a huge salad. I didn't want my mom to feel like she needed to cook again after she had already eaten. I was excited to try to be more connected with my food and the process from beginning to end.

I read about a practice that Deepak Chopra described as conscious eating and intentional chewing. He described staying in the present moment. He details the importance of eating healthy whole foods to nurture and feed our bodies. He describes how to stay connected while we eat. I practiced my conscious connection to try to reduce some stress and build a break for my body, mind, and spirit.

My mind was focused on using water to rinse the vegetables, the feeling of the floor under my feet, the countertop under the cutting board, the knife in my hand, and the color of the food as it was being peeled, sliced, and chopped, the texture and the smell.

I thought about what I had learned about the color of foods and how the color is indicative of how the food heals and supports my body. The red beets healed and supported my blood and heart. The orange carrot helped keep my eyes strong. The creamy green avocado removed my sugar craving and gave my hair and skin a healthy glow. The dark green spinach built muscle and cleansed my colon. The sunflower seeds and flax added protein. The smell of the fresh vegetables reached my nose, and I inhaled as I was sitting down at a clear, uncluttered table to stay present.

I felt the cool granite tile under my hands when I picked up the bowl and fork. Gratitude for the beautiful food grown by the sun to become a melody of energy for my body. I thanked the clean water that nurtured the vegetables and the healthy earth for providing the nutrients for them to grow. I felt the fork in my hand. I saw the pleasing color of the bowl holding my salad. I did a deliberate loading on the fork. I tasted each ingredient of the salad. I consciously chewed the food and swallowed.

My mom saw what I was doing and asked me about it, "Janna, why are you eating so strangely?"

I'm practicing conscientious eating, the thing Deepak talked about in his book, remember? I'm trying to be connected to my food and time, hoping it will reduce my stress."

"Oh. Is it working?" she asked.

"I think so; I feel happier right now."

"It looks like you're meditating while you eat."

"I kind of am, I guess." I take a big breath in then I exhale. "Yup, I feel better," I say.

I noticed when I started eating highly processed foods, the desire for the color, texture, and taste of whole foods dims. My palate is quick to regain the taste for whole foods again when I eat them. It's always good to check in with my consciousness about how healthfully I'm eating.

I periodically reviewed my food habits. I tried to adjust and move closer to a more nutritious, whole foods plant-based diet. I asked myself these questions: How much sugar am I consuming? How much oil? How many processed meals have I eaten lately? How am I congruent with my values about food? Then, when and where I could, I tweaked it. Spring and Fall are good times to do a mental inventory. They are natural times of change, and nature's visual change helps spur me along.

The struggle I experienced with the lack of connection with my dad bothered me. I realize when I fail to connect with people, I punish myself with ruthless, self-harming thoughts. I had to learn to navigate my mistakes so I could change and grow.

Often, I would shut down and intentionally forget the interaction so I wouldn't become obsessed with the failed connection. When I remembered and accepted a situation, I learned from my experience.

I need to stop punishing myself with shame when I make a mistake. I'm not sure how to change this, but I'll learn.

Connection will be a focus in my life forever. It will drive my goals, beliefs, and actions. I believed connection was the foundation on which I would build my life.

Chapter Thirty-Six
Respect

Many years ago, my mom and I had a week-long conversation about respect. "Respect must be earned." She stated adamantly.

"What if respect is not earned but given because I'm a respectful person?" I replied.

"I think each generation becomes less respectful; I'm appalled at how young kids talk to people." She said.

"What do you think changed?" I asked.

"My generation, the Baby Boomers, were heavily influenced by radio and TV. However, my parents and family still had high involvement and were sticklers for what behaviors equaled respect. I was expected to have eye contact; there was no talking back, and I was doing as I was told. Now kids have computers, social media, video games, and the Web. Kids are influenced by anything on a screen. As much as some parents try, everyone is busy trying to pay bills, and kids are influenced by so much parents can't control." She explained.

I replied, "I remember Grandma Fran came to visit, and we were all in the car together, and she asked Jordan a question. His response was something he heard from watching Johnny Bravo. Grandma Fran was upset and told him not to be sassy. I was upset at how he responded, too. I started monitoring their television shows more closely. I think that's when I decided to get rid of their Nintendo. When I investigated Jonny Bravo, I was angry they marketed it on children's TV and labeled it youth humor or entertainment. I do think teaching behavior to children is important. However, I would emphasize it is taught so they understand they are only responsible for themselves. I also believe it's important to teach without shame or blame. I think expecting others to earn respect is bound to fail. When they don't earn respect, they're labeled and blamed. I can only be who I decide to be in this world. I decided to respect all people because I have decided to be respectable." I said.

When we talked about how my children grew up and how they were influenced, it seemed like they were exposed to sarcasm, violence, and cheeky behaviors through TV, video games, and computers. One of my changed beliefs was that I grew up being told respect is earned. I wanted to give all people respect because I'm a respectful person. *I'm responsible for myself and how I behave.*

On October 16, 2015, my dad died. After a life of heavy drinking and smoking his health declined. He experienced multiple mini-strokes and episodes of losing time, and he couldn't walk well. While visiting a friend in North Dakota, he had a heart attack.

I received a call from the hospital in the middle of the night. They needed permission from a family member to do emergency surgery. His body continued failing after the heart attack and surgery. The final event was while he was in a nursing home that was overcrowded and understaffed, and he fell and broke his hip. I decided it was time for hospice to be involved. He was pale and emaciated. I could see his body's desire to let go of this life. I saw no point in doing surgery for a body that was ready to go. He confirmed my decision and told the hospice people he was ready. He was only concerned about whether he would experience pain. The hospice worker assured him, "It will be as easy as falling asleep." He liked that.

As I left the hospital, the weight of making the decision was overwhelming. I didn't make it to my car. I sat on a berm, put my head between my legs, and sobbed. My mom sat next to me in silence with her hand on my back. I wept for about ten minutes. Then I stood up and walked to the car.

The next day, while he was in the hospital, my brothers, Dylan and I all held hands around his bed and said the Lord's Prayer. It's a precious memory. He became tearful and communicated his appreciation through his eyes. He was never verbose with his love and affection, but it was there I saw it. I realize today how important this moment was for him and me.

He died a few days later. My mom was by his side for the whole process. I couldn't make myself be there. I was still mad at God. My life still felt hard and unfair. I struggled to grieve for my dad. He hadn't been a physical presence in my life. The one exception to the grief was when I was at a hockey game. He had started to take Dylan and me to see EHL hockey games, and he never missed one of my boys' games if he could be there.

I remember sitting in the stands at the first game after he passed. I felt so alone and sad. I did find time to grieve for my dad, but it was a few years after he passed. I finally saw how he loved me, then I felt my loss. It still bubbles up sometimes when I'm at a game.

In November, right before Thanksgiving break, the district manager at the call center, Tabitha, was screaming at me and shaming me. She accused me of having black-and-white thinking and told me I was failing at my job. She was angry because I called the staff "my interpreters." I stopped listening after that.

It was abusive and hurtful. I didn't know how to respond, so I reacted. I hung up the phone and went home.

While on Thanksgiving break, I was obsessed with how to handle it. I had the support of my mom, but I realized I had very few friends in Colorado, and I had no Higher Power. Control was driving the bus of life again.

I decided to call a meeting with Tabitha and her boss. During the meeting, I planned to use the communication techniques I learned from The Caron Foundation and Ken. I thought the meeting went okay, but the next week, I was put on probation for the mistakes I'd made. I felt resentful and afraid.

Three months after my dad's death, Tom's dad died. I was not told until much later he had passed away, but I saw how negatively these two significant losses impacted my youngest son, Dylan.

Dylan was close to my dad in the last year of his life, and he was very close to his paternal grandfather. My boys called him Pop Pop. He looked like Santa Claus. He was a short, heavy-set man with a long white beard and a big laugh. He grew up in Brooklyn on Flatbush Avenue. He loved books and watching the news, and his addiction was food. He had a tattoo on his upper arm of dice (snake eyes). Under the dice were the words, *born to lose*. His tattoo was from his time in the military. He loved my boys and spent time reading books to them. When he pronounced my name with his accent, it sounded like "Janner." When I hear a New York accent, I think of Pop Pop. He had PTSD.

Dylan started drinking and using drugs and it was destructive to his life and mine. I'll always be grateful I had an enormous box of tools from my many years of sobriety.

My mom and I had started the process of buying a condo together. We found one that met all our needs. Dylan and I each had a bedroom, and there was a shared bathroom upstairs. KC Jones, our dog, now had a fenced backyard.

Then, an employee who had been angry I was promoted, was giving me a hard time. In front of another manager, after he left, I flipped him off. She told Tabitha and I was fired. He had not seen it, but I was disrespectful to him.

In my family, growing up, we all flipped each other off. It wasn't a big deal. I learned once again that my childhood behavior hadn't served me well as an adult. I felt terrified of the financial loss, and I was ashamed I'd allowed disrespect, resentment, and pride to dictate my behavior.

Later, I used this experience to become more realistic about my thoughts and beliefs, which led to my situation. I wished I'd gone to human resources after Tabitha shamed me. I wasn't guilty of all her accusations, but I was guilty of some of them. Out of my shame, I didn't believe I deserved protection from her abuse. I recognized my life would become extremely stressful and challenging if I stayed at a job where my direct boss didn't like me. I learned I had to start making choices to support my inner peace and health.

I began to build a new support system. I started praying and asking God for help. I knew I had to let go of my blame toward my Higher Power and the control of others. I would choose to trust in God, clean house, and finally be happy during the upcoming years.

Chapter Thirty-Seven
Trust in God

I focused on trust in God from 2016 to 2017. I had to get busy and connect with a Higher Power. It was critical I didn't give credit or blame for what was happening in my life. I wanted to connect with a Higher Power that was Love. That simple Love. Life was going to happen, and I had to stop believing a Higher Power would change anything. From now on, my commitment will be to a Loving Tree, the Stars in the Sky, or the Love I feel toward Animals. I wouldn't blame the Tree, Sky or Animals for what was happening in my life. I'd believe the same for my Higher Power. I needed a secure *relationship* with something greater than myself that I could trust. Constant Love. I had begun with the simplicity of a Tree, then somehow tried to get my Higher Power to control things, and now I would go back to the Tree. Simple.

When I first learned humans breathe out precisely what plants breathe in, and plants breathe out exactly what humans breathe in, I immediately felt excited. This was evidence of something greater than myself. The love of the whole Universe in connection with each other. Plants and humans need each other to survive. Our structures mirror each other. Humans have a body, arms, blood, and legs. Trees have a trunk and branches, phloem, and roots. Both are made of carbon cells and need the sun, water, vitamins, and minerals from the Earth. We need each other to sustain life. These are the synchronicities of a loving God.

There was a lot of codependency and enmeshment between my mom and me. I couldn't be honest with myself about the many ways I felt hurt and abandoned by her in my youth, and I wasn't willing to look at the dysfunction of our relationship. My mom was more of a best friend and business partner than a parent, and if we disagreed about topics, it was difficult for her. I rarely expressed disagreement. When I did, it felt scary and uncomfortable. I spent most of my free time with her.

My mom had found a man on YouTube named Bob Wells. He interviewed people living in recreational vehicles (RVs) on the road. It was fascinating. She watched all his interviews. I would join in when I wasn't at work or out with friends. We would pause the interview and talk about altering what they said to make it work for us. My mom dreamed of selling all her possessions and traveling in an RV to see America. We looked at RVs and talked about how we could make it happen. We were preparing for a much simpler lifestyle. All of the people Bob interviewed talked about their freedom. This idea appealed to both my mom and me, and we watched everything she found on the subject. It was interesting and exciting.

My son's addiction was ramping up, and my mom had disagreed several times about how I was handling it. I knew I had to be supportive and loving of my son. My mom was struggling to see how kindness and tolerance could work. She didn't understand my approach. She believed in control and punishment. She called it "tough love," There was often stress and tension between us. I'd taken the kindness and tolerance approach with Tom in his addiction when we were getting our divorce, and I felt proud of the way I handled most of it; I knew it could work. I remained kind and tolerant toward Dylan. I added compassion and love to the recipe. When he was destructive and violent, I reminded myself he was sick with his addiction.

I wasn't loving enough when Jordan began going through a time of underaged use, nor did I have compassion. I was hurt and angry which didn't work well. My successes and failures empowered me to know the course I wanted to take. Love and support were the keys to getting through this difficult experience.

Creating structure helped me relinquish control and provided a framework for my inner security. Most of all, I used the tools I learned in my own life to remain congruent with my thoughts, feelings, and actions. At some point, as I thought about my approach, I remember thinking *when I control other people, I'm sending them the message they can't be successful on their own, which is shaming.*

Addiction can be a long up-and-down journey for the addict and the people who love them. When I saw a change in his personality, I knew he was using drugs again. He would stop communicating with me, and no longer keep his word about going to hockey games and coming home. He would no longer have a connection to me or his own life.

We had a couple of years of home drug testing, creating boundaries, calls from the police late at night, court dates, payments, and probation officer meetings. I showed up for it all. I was steady like a tree. I knew this was something I must show up for to support my son. That was my goal. I needed to be present with love and compassion in tow. My structure was, *how would I treat him if this was cancer?*

One day, I went through his room and removed all alcohol, drugs, lighters, pipes, and glass bongs. If this was cancer, I would be removing pesticide-laden foods, sugar, meat, and anything deemed a carcinogen. Dylan was a minor, and I was responsible for him. I had always maintained a home that was safe from alcohol and drugs. That would remain the same. No alcohol, drugs, or tobacco. He was *furious*. He confronted me with all his anger.

"Janna! Where is my stuff?" Dylan yelled.

I walked to the bottom of the steps and looked up. Dylan stood at the top of the stairs with rage on his face. "Where is my stuff?!" He yelled again.

"Do you mean your drugs, alcohol, lighters, and bongs?" I said calmly.

He paused. "Yes! My Stuff!" he yelled with an emphasis on the word "my."

"I removed anything that is illegal for you to have in order to maintain a safe space. Those are the boundaries in our home."

"Where is my glass bull? That was expensive! I do not use it for drugs! It's not even mine!"

"I used a hammer and shattered the bong, then I threw it away," I explained.

He came down the stairs in a flash. Opened the glass door, grabbed an angel-shaped Willow figurine, and said, "If you steal and break my stuff, I'm going to break your stuff."

Willows are porcelain figurines; they look like carved wood or trees. I had many angels and some people pieces. They were displayed in the bottom of my Grandma Alices' clock cabinet. It was located in the living room, at the bottom of the steps, near the front door of our home.

My mom was standing in the kitchen a few feet away. She would be a witness to our moment. I heard her take a shocked breath. Then I took a step back, pulled my shoulders back, and I took a calming breath. I thought *This is it. He needs to know you love him.*

He threw the angel on the tile floor. "Crash" it shattered. Then he reached in and grabbed another one. As he was grabbing them and breaking them, I was standing in front of him saying, "I love you more than the angel you just broke. You and your health are more important to me than the Willows you are breaking. I will be here to keep you safe. I love you."

I kept saying it over and over in a calm, steady voice. I looked him in the eyes with all my momma-bear love as I told him these words. I mirrored him with the words, "The angel you just broke," it acknowledged I was present and saw him. It returned some power back to him. Then I repeated my mantra several times. "I love you more than the angel you just broke. You and your health are more important to me than the Willows you are breaking. I will be here to keep you safe. I love you."

I watched him stop breathing while he looked at the floor; I heard him catch his breath and suck in air. He looked up and looked into my eyes; his own eyes began to fill with tears. He gave up and stormed out the door. My mother still stood in the kitchen, and she was silent.

I cleaned up the shattered ceramic pieces, and it was over. I thought about how I wasn't able to be this supportive, kind, loving Mom to Jordan while he struggled with his underage use. I had learned how to have empathy and I had grown. I had become the mother I wanted for myself. I went upstairs to my room and sat in my rocking chair.

Breathe. Meditate. Pray. Love.

During the years of addiction, several nights I was awoken by the sound of Dylan throwing up. I often didn't know if it was drugs, food poisoning, or flu. When he was disrespectful, I didn't know if it was teenage brain or withdrawal. It was an incredibly difficult time to navigate my thoughts and feelings. I focused on congruency. I leaned into my support team and the Universe. I stayed committed to knowing I could trust my Higher Power.

I don't know the future, and I accept what is true right now. It might look different at another time, but right now, this is what I know.

I tried hard to avoid telling myself stories, I focused on the facts. I kept praying and meditating and stayed connected to friends I knew understood and could support my approach. I didn't share information with people who blamed and shamed Dylan for his illness.

I used my time when he was not home, meditating and remembering what I felt and experienced when I was an active addict at his age. I thought about what worked and what didn't work.

I asked myself *what would I have needed to support a change in my behavior from my parents.* The answer I heard was *stability, love, and support.*

Then I asked myself *what does stability look like?* The answer was *a safe place to come with food and a clean bed.*

Then I asked myself *what does support look like?* The solution for this situation was boundaries and structure.

Then I asked myself *what does love look like?* The answer was *compassion and acceptance.*

I'm not sure I would have been able to pull it off if I was still culpable myself. I was sober, I knew I could be stable, supportive, and loving.

What could I do to support Dylan? How can I keep him safe, healthy, and accountable? How can I implement boundaries? Acceptance of each moment helped me have the energy to take action. *Stay in compassion, he is sick. Be kind, Be loving, Be supportive.*

I remember one time Dylan was using heavily and staying out all night. My mom was pressuring me to lock him out of our house. I went up to my bedroom. I prayed and meditated. I called a support person. My friend reminded me if I locked him out, I diminished his safe options.

I had been drug testing him, and he had started refusing to comply. He looked like an addict, with dirty, unkempt clothes and bloodshot eyes. I felt worried for his life.

I kept asking myself *if he had cancer, how would I treat him? I would do everything in my power to keep him safe.*

I began to look into treatment options for Dylan. I found an amazing outdoor wilderness treatment experience I wanted to send him to. I knew I wasn't able or willing to pay 30 – 40 thousand dollars for him to go to treatment.

I did all I could to keep him in hockey. It was a healthy, safe place for him. I consulted with his coach about my plan and his illness. I shared my perspective and ideas. I was specific with people about what I needed from them.

The message to the team at the beginning of the year was if a person missed a game for no reason, the coach would bench them. I asked the coach to follow through with his missed game rule with love and a clear boundary. I made a commitment to

Coach that I wouldn't make excuses and cover up Dylan's behavior.

I only remember Dylan missing one game. The coach clarified they had to show up for the benched game and support their team. Dylan looked angry while he sat on the bench, and I imagined it was hard. He wasn't picked on or shamed. He was asked what had happened. He was seen, heard, and encouraged to show up for the rest of the season. That was love. It was holding someone accountable for their behavior without shaming or punishing them. I learned from this experience too.

Eventually, Dylan was brought into the legal system. *Is this an answered prayer? This is the wisdom of all the people who have been working with young addicts for many years. Now he will be held accountable, and it may open doors for help and support.*

I called Tom to talk to him about the legal system and possibly paying for treatment. "Tom, Dylan's in trouble. He's using drugs and drinking. I feel afraid. I think he needs treatment."

"I heard you told his probation officer he ran away. That is total betrayal, what a fucked-up thing to do." He retorted.

After our conversation, I accepted Tom would be unable to give me any support. I continued to call Tom and inform him about the facts. My intention was to keep the calls very brief and to the point, then I hung up.

As Dylan's behavior became sicker, I became more creative. I couldn't afford the awesome treatment program, but I was his mother, and I had been sober for a long time. I used my tools to love and care for my sick son. I knew I had to trust in God and in myself. I prayed and meditated. I didn't pray for anything to be changed or controlled. I prayed for intuitive thoughts to guide my actions. Then, I meditated and listened. I thought of something Tom told me. He said, "One of the times I was sent to treatment after a long run, I remember how much I loved having a clean, safe place to lay my head. I was exhausted." Tom's mom no longer had the authority to help him in this way. I still had the authority to help Dylan.

I began to form a new plan. *I can make his room more like a treatment center room. Is that kind? Compassionate and loving? Yes. Keep it Simple. Meet his basic needs.* Then, I knew what I had to do.

I used my anxious, fearful energy to get busy. I took all his possessions and put them in a storage unit for $30.00/month. I took off the door to his room that went to storage. I removed any valuable things I cared about and put them in storage too. On the bottom of his bed, I stacked three clean folded white t-shirts, one pair of black jeans, five white socks, five pairs of underwear, and one pair of black shoes. I made his bed with a pillow, a sheet, and a blanket. This made it possible for me to report what he could be wearing to his probation officer if he didn't come home. It removed the fancy clothes he wore to impress other kids, and it wasn't enough clean clothes for him to be gone very long. I knew he liked clean clothes and fancy accessories.

What gave me an advantage over treatment was that I had known my child all his life. I knew what motivated him and what he didn't care about. I loved him like a mama bear loves her cub. I realized he could trade clothes or buy new clothes, but here is the thing about an addict, all their time, money, and energy are used to get and use drugs. The clothes approach was a loving, soft structure for both him and me.

I left the Willows in their case. When Dylan broke the Willows, I became very clear that possessions mean very little to me in comparison to the people in my life. I no longer felt as attached to things unless they had a connection to people.

I told him my plan when he came home, "All of your belongings are in a safe place. You can earn them back with compliance and respect. These are my boundaries: going to school on time every day, being ready and on time for hockey games, speaking to adults with respect, and submitting to random drug tests when asked. Remaining clean and sober while living at our home," I explained.

I bought a journal and documented the drug test results and what I saw and thought. It was like the Pensive in *Harry Potter*. The journal allowed me to look back and be more explicit about what actions I implemented and the timeline of events with Dylan. The journaling helped me support myself through the process. I kept better clarity when I needed to remember the past for corrections in the future. I supported myself. Then, I could go forward when I needed to get busy.

I bought a package of twelve six-panel urine cards. I liked the one that tests for marijuana, opiates, PCP, cocaine, methamphetamine, and amphetamine. I also bought a urine collecting cup with a thermometer on the side. This ensures that the urine is fresh and at body temperature. I was careful to do the random tests in the morning, so he had less chance to deceive the test. I read on a website that people with addiction will get a clean friend to pee in a jar and pour it into a bag, tape the bag to the backside of a sink and hide it in the bathroom. Then use that if they have privacy when they peed. I stood in the doorway with my back turned. I determined what was earned with each test, and that was how he earned his belongings back.

In hindsight, if I had planned better and known more, I would have communicated to him the structure more clearly. I was researching and making the plan as his disease progressed, parts of it were clumsy and not well done. I did the best I could and I took the shot.

"You miss 100% of the shots you never take." Wayne Gretzky

One evening, he was out past the curfew I had set for him. My mom was pressuring me to lock him out of the house, but that felt scary to me. I was unsure why I didn't like the idea. I went up to my bedroom and sat in my rocking chair to meditate. As I rocked and chanted, I became clear my loving safe approach didn't include him getting locked out of the safe place he could come.

If he had cancer, I would not lock him out of the house.

As I was meditating, I heard him trying to get into the house. I waited. Then I heard nothing. *The door must be locked!*

I ran downstairs and he was no longer near the house. *What if he dies because he didn't have a safe option tonight?*

I grabbed my keys and tried to find him; I looked for about 20 min. *Please God, keep him safe.*

When I arrived home, he was sitting at the picnic table outside. "Hi, Dylan." I said relieved.

"Hey."

"I'm glad you're home and you're safe. I felt afraid for your safety tonight. Doing drugs is life-threatening."

He looked down at the ground but didn't respond.

"I love you," I said. No response.

"Can you look at my eyes, please? You missed your curfew. What happened?"

He just shrugged. I could see the emotion in his eyes.

"Okay, it's late. I would appreciate it if we could talk in the morning."

There were a lot of one-sided conversations. I tried to always reiterate I loved him, and I wanted him to be safe. I maintained the parent role with the authority to decide love over punishment. Kindness over criticism. Respect over shame. I also focused on verbal praise and eye contact with the intention to build trust and connection. It was hard. I stayed consistent and kept prayer and meditation practices twice a day.

When the law became involved, I was able to tell the courts about the times I tested him and when he was clean. I had a record in my journal.

At one point, I had to clarify with Dylan, "A refusal is equivalent to a positive drug test result." He had refused, I accepted it without comment and marked it as a 'hot' in my journal.

Addiction is living a life of the false self. It takes a toll on our hearts. It's also exhausting. I was not in control, and I gave myself structure and boundaries to remain safe and present in what was happening. *I was growing and learning.*

Dylan was clean and sober for a short time. Then he relapsed and ran away. Hockey was over and he had lost both grandpas close together. The stress of school and grief were too much.

"Dylan, are you high?" I asked him one day after school.

"What does it matter, Mom? Really."

"The boundary is you have to be clean and sober to live in this house, Dylan."

"Okay."

It was May so school was almost over, hockey season was done, and Dylan was in a dark place once again.

When I told him he had to be clean and sober to live in our home, he heard he was kicked out. We had different perspectives.

He had met a new friend I didn't know. The new friend's mother let Dylan move in without communicating with me. I had no idea where Dylan was, if he was safe, or how he was doing. *What if he gets into a car accident and I never see my son alive again?* My head was spinning. I knew this was a real possibility. I watched it happen 25 years ago. I called his skateboarding friends and they told me he was safe. They had seen him at the parks. They didn't know where he was staying but they promised to keep an eye on him.

Later when Dylan came home, I felt angry and disappointed about the behavior of the unknown mother. I probably would have sued her for interfering with my program if I had the means. I had to pray for her for weeks to let go of my resentment and anger. I worked hard to find acceptance. I realized this was a person suffering from her own disease. I realized my own mother had acted in a similar way long ago. *I'm grateful for the work I have done and for who I am.*

In June of 2017, my younger brother moved from Colorado to Phoenix, Arizona. My mom encouraged him to go. Jordan was also planning to move to Phoenix, Arizona. He had been accepted to the Motorcycle Mechanics Institute (MMI).

Later that month, I went to a doctor's appointment with my mom. She began coughing in November, and she hadn't felt good for months. She had an MRI in early May and was getting the results at the appointment. She asked me to come with her. In mid-June, my mom set up an appointment to see her lawyer before we went to the Doctor's appointment. When we arrived, the lawyer's secretary took us back to the big conference room, with the large leather chairs and mahogany table for 20.

"Hi Ann, I have your will is all set."

"Hi, Patty. Okay." Patty sat across from my mom and me.

"The only thing you need to decide is if Janna will be the executor, too." My mom looked at me.

"What?" I said, finally paying attention.

My mom stared into my eyes and said, "Janna, I am thinking about making you the executor of my estate. You'll inherit all my personal belongings, and I know you'll distribute them appropriately. You're the only one who lives in Colorado. So I think you should be the executor of the estate. I know it's a lot of responsibility."

I sat in the room as it spun around me. *Why is she putting it all on me? This is too much. It sucks. I don't want to be here. What's going on?* "Okay, mom," I said as I looked into her eyes.

"Janna, I'll need you to sign some paperwork." Patty directed.

When we left, I had a sick nervousness rolling through my intestines. *This is turning into a terrible day.* We arrived at the doctor's office, and the nurse brought us back to the room. *No waiting is bad,* my mind remembered.

The doctor explained, "Your cancer has metastasized to your liver."

He showed us the MRI of her liver. It was dark black on two-thirds of the outer edge. The Doctor was talking to my mom about her cancer. I was going to sob, "Excuse me." I said as I ran to the bathroom. I sat on the toilet with my pants on and my head in my hands and cried silently. Then I splashed some water on my face and went back into the room to support my mom.

She was told to get her affairs in order. They told her she had months to years left. She did not. She lived forty-eight days from the appointment.

I was her primary caregiver. I put together a team of people to support and give me breaks. They called themselves Team Ann. They were absolutely incredible. I learned a lot from all of them. They would come to the house and visit with my mom while I worked, exercised, visited with my support group, did household chores, and cried.

I made time to walk and cry. I would let myself take a 5-minute break to cry as I needed. Three minutes to cry and two minutes to let the redness around my eyes and face fade.

I'm not a natural caregiver. My parents both knew this. I made mistakes, and I did the best I could for them at that time.

My mother invited her friend from her hometown in Nebraska to come and be with her. She had helped others crossover and was a Registered Nurse Assistant. This friend didn't like me and was not subtle about it. I was respectful to her. When I look back at the forty-eight days, I know it was uncomfortable for me to have her there. I felt I had to leave when she came and find other things to do. I wanted to spend time with my mom. I reminded myself I wasn't in control; it was my mom's request, so I honored it. I was proud of my maturity to accept her and make a place for her. She stayed in Dylan's nearly empty room. I had not seen or heard from Dylan in a few weeks.

During the year of trust, I learned to follow my intuition more. I learned that I'm not in control of what happens in life, nor is God. I'm only able to choose how I feel and respond to it. I learned that my Higher Power isn't to be blamed when difficult experiences happen. How things unfold isn't mine to judge. I was learning how to trust the greater good of the Universe. I was going to be an orphan soon. Grief was coming, and once again, I would experience growth in amazing ways.

My new focus for the upcoming year would be "clean house." It was perfect. Mom and I watched all those videos with Bob Wells and the RV freedom gang. Plan B was forming.

I had an amazing year learning to trust my Higher Power through it all.

Chapter Thirty-Eight
Clean House

My mom crossed over on July 31, 2017. Grief took over my life. I was either numb, angry, sad, or in total acceptance, and it changed like the waves coming onto the shore of a beach. Some waves were huge and took me to my knees; some were small, and I was able to manage them.

My mom was one of the brightest researchers I have ever known. When one of us learned a new bit of information, she researched. Then, we would talk for hours about what we thought, didn't understand, and wanted to learn more about.

She believed her whole foods plant-based diet added years to her life. She was the person I was connected with daily, and we walked the sober vegan journey together for nine years.

During her second experience with cancer, she chose CBD, marijuana, and finally, with the aid of hospice, morphine to manage her pain. During her final 48 days, she shared information she wanted me to know, asked me questions she was curious about, and planned her celebration of life. She told me what songs she wanted played, found the location, and told me what possessions to display.

I leaned on my friends. They were very supportive, and many invited me into their lives, which gave me a break. *I'm grateful.*

My mom believed years of animal products, pesticides, arsenic-laden water, and sugar caused cancer in her body. In addition to having root canals on the intestinal meridian in her mouth. She believed the whole foods plant-based eating prevented her from dying earlier, like her sister (50s) and her brother (60s). She felt betrayed by her cancerous body and wasn't ready to go. In the end, she had no choice.

On July 28, 2017, the police called to let me know they had picked up Dylan, and he was at the detention center. It was about four o'clock in the morning.

After I hung up the phone, I heard the water running in my mother's bathroom on the monitor I used to listen to her at night. I went downstairs to check on my mom. Her frail, skinny, weak body was propped up against the counter, surrounded by the walker in her bathroom, and she was trying to brush her teeth.

"Good morning. What are you doing?" I said.

"Getting ready to visit Dylan." *She must have been waiting for this.*

"Oh." *I cannot carry or support her if she falls; we have such a big day. How can I navigate this? Gentle. Kind. Gentle. Kind. Her nurse friend can help with the lifting and support.*

"Okay, I know you want to see Dylan. However, your brother and sister-in-law are coming to visit you, and your nurse friend will be here later. Let's wait until your friend comes, and she can help us go see Dylan."

"Okay," my mom replied dejectedly. I helped her get into the shower and put on clean clothes. Then we sat together on the couch and talked. After our family left, my mom asked if I'd help her get into bed. She never got out of bed again. She didn't get to see Dylan.

When loved ones begin to actively cross over, it's hard to know which decisions will be "thank god" and which decisions will be "darn it, I wish I'd known." I wish I had known and taken her to see Dylan. I know I made the safest decision, so I don't have any regrets.

On July 29, at about two in the morning. I went into my mom's room to give her a dose of morphine. When I entered her room, it was freezing, and the air was thick. I could feel a blackness. It made me freeze where I was standing at the foot of her bed. I knew I couldn't enter her room. I felt goosebumps and cold energy.

I decided she'd miss this dose of morphine. I went back to bed, but I didn't sleep. I felt disturbed by what I'd experienced. I thought death was peaceful and easy, like letting go. I felt confused and afraid. When I shared this story with her nurse assistant friend the next day, she said, "Oh, you interrupted their meeting." I thought about a book called *Embraced by the Light* by Betty J. Eadie, which I read in 1992. Then again, more recently, when I struggled with my Higher Power. This book talked about the meetings that the other side had to help a person cross over. I always imagined these meetings were warm and full of bright, supportive light. I realized that isn't the case for living human intruders. This experience led me to believe my mom must have been fighting to stay. I thought it would be good to let her know her three children were okay and that it was time to surrender.

I was given permission from the detention center for Dylan to have a Facetime call. My mom couldn't respond, but I hoped that Dylan would have closure when saying goodbye and that my mom would hear his voice. *I hope I made the right decision.* I tried to reach Jordan, but he didn't return my calls.

On the night of July 30, Sean came to my home. Chad was on FaceTime, and we all told my mother it was time to go. We told her we'd be okay. We said "goodbye" and told her how much we loved her. Then Chad and I prayed the Serenity Prayer together.

At 2 in the morning, on July 31, 2017, I woke up and gave my mom another dose of morphine. The nurse friend woke me up at 4 a.m. and told me she was gone.

I didn't cry or touch her. She looked the same as she had for the past two days. Her body seemed devoid of any self or spirit. I called my older brother at his hotel and asked him to come to the house. Then I called the funeral home where my mom had made arrangements. Sean and the funeral home people arrived at about 6:00 a.m. Sean and Mom's friend said their final goodbyes, and they all left.

I lay in my soft, warm bed for about an hour; then I prepared for court with Dylan. He had a hearing to decide if he would be released. I asked Dylan's lawyer if I could go into the holding cell to tell him his grandmother had passed away a few hours earlier. I was escorted back behind the wall to a concrete holding cell in the courthouse. I sat beside Dylan and said, "Grandma Ann is gone." Then I put my arms around him. It was a difficult day for us both.

Thankfully, I had a friend who came to support me. Also, I was still in shock, so I could do what needed to be done. Dylan wasn't released for another week. I don't remember much about this week. I know I felt totally alone.

I've learned that my first reaction to grief is a pause. I imagine the slowing of time has to do with trauma chemicals in my body, like when a person is injured physically. Grief is an injury that draws no blood and leaves no visible wound. It took a while for the numbness of shock to abate. When the shock wore off, the tears and crying came on strong and fast.

In her final days, my mom and I had planned her celebration of life together. I knew it was time to get busy. Once again, I had so much support from my friends. I organized and arranged her celebration just as we planned. My mom would have loved it.

Dylan wanted to do something special for his Grandma Ann, so he and I discussed his idea during dinner after his release. He wanted to do a butterfly release at her service. She loved butterflies, which would be the perfect way for her grandchildren to honor their relationship. I bought seventy butterflies for her seventy years of life. Twenty-six were bigger than the others to honor her twenty-six years of sobriety. Her grandkids at the celebration did the release. It was beautiful. I often have butterflies flying around me when I am outside now. I always say "Hi" to my mom when they appear.

I lost my best friend, my business partner, and my mom on the same day at the same moment. It has been the most challenging experience of my life thus far. I realize now that I was aware of my feelings without the benefit of being attached to myself. I believe this was part of why I struggled for so many years in grief. Feeling grief without inner attachment and self-love is never resolved. It gets stuck like lost socks in a dryer.

My mom was sober, vegan, and brilliant. She was a force. I missed my best friend. I started cleaning our house.

On December 21, 2017, six months later, Tom died of a drug overdose. It was too much. More people loved me on the other side than on this one. I wanted to be on the other side with them. I wanted my grief and pain to end. The feeling of being alone permeated my whole life. I didn't drink, and I kept leaning on my wonderful friends.

I was just starting to get back on my feet from losing my mom, and now I felt like a widow. Tom and I weren't married, but I was still connected to him, through our children, through my heart, through our eighteen years together. Whenever I was with our children, I saw his spirit and energy, which comforted me.

About a week before Tom passed, he called me. "Hi, Tom, what's up?" I answered my cell phone.

"What are you doing? Do you have a minute?"

"Sure, I'm getting ready to drive to the Tiny Home Show, so I can talk as long as the cell tower gods allow it."

"Oh, cool. I wanted to talk to you about the boys."

"Okay, what about?"

"Are you keeping in touch with Jordan?"

"Yes, as much as he'll allow. He doesn't always want to talk to me."

"Please keep in touch with him. He doesn't always show it, but he worries and holds a lot of feelings inside."

"Yeah, he's like a turtle. Dylan pointed that out to me one time. He joked that maybe that was the reason he loves turtles so much."

"Yeah, speaking of Dylan, he needs you too. I know he has been giving you a rough time, but you're a good mother, and he knows that. Stick close to him." It was the first time I heard Tom talk in this way. I felt his love for our boys and his support and love for me.

"I'll always do my best for our sons; they are the most important people in my life."

We talked for an hour and a half. It was an excellent connection, and we had a fantastic conversation. He told me he planned to move to New York City and work for an ex-girlfriend's father repairing refrigerators. He said he was ready to leave the town he had lived in for over twenty-five years. I remember thinking New York City was not a good idea, but I was no longer in a place where I could make suggestions about his life. At one point, I thought about asking him to move to Colorado. I had a huge empty condo, and it would have been nice for Dylan to be close to his dad. *Don't do it; if he's using, he brings all the chaos with him. You have your hands full already.*

On December 21, I had a dream that Tom came to me. We were making love. It was familiar, comfortable, and wonderful. He told me, "I'll always love you." I woke up a little shaken. I rarely dreamed of him, and it felt so real.

On my way to work, one of the men who had taken Tommy to treatment all those years earlier called me and asked me how I was doing. I replied, "What's wrong?" He told me he was trying to confirm that Tommy was gone. He'd seen a post on Facebook that morning. I knew it was true before anyone confirmed it. My dream was all the confirmation I needed.

I went to work and cried with a coworker. He had lost a family member recently and was very supportive. He sat with me while I called the coroner from our former town in Pennsylvania to get confirmation. It was confirmed. I was heartbroken. I felt numb. Again.

Ed, Tom's brother, invited me to participate in the service and helped make the arrangements. He told me I'd always be his sister, and I was the best part of Tom's life. I felt so much love from him. My friends rallied around me, and I received love and comfort.

In January, I was having a tough time with wanting to live. I shared this with some friends. One of them, a man I respected, could see how much I was struggling. He came up to me, hugged me, and said, "I love you." It was unexpected, intimate, and authentic. When I remembered his hug and love, I knew I could get through another dark night because I had a moment of affection, love, and connection with another human.

At one time, Tom had known everything about my life. Then, I lived with my mom, who also witnessed my day-to-day events. We shared movies, TV programs, and books, and we talked about our thoughts and feelings every day. I realized that people who knew the small details of my daily life and my history with them were what I missed the most. This is grief.

There was no person left who knew me before I knew myself, was there for the birth of both my children, would sit in the front row of my children's weddings with me to remember joyful things about them as babies and toddlers and children, to put their arms around me and say, "I love you each morning and night."

I let the despair and grief have me. I cried so much that I had no eyelashes for a couple of years. I couldn't focus enough to be able to work, and I wasn't connected to myself yet. It was a lonely, difficult time in my life.

I didn't drink. I had developed great habits and stayed true to my values while I grieved. The solution was to learn to love me. Then, I needed to become attached or connected to myself. I knew this was the "belonging" Brené Brown talked about in the book *Daring Greatly*.

At times, I have felt alone on the sober vegan path. The general world eats meat and drinks alcohol, and the world can seem judgmental and shaming.

In March 2017, I sold my condo, paid off debt, and moved into a 35-foot fifth-wheel RV I bought for $11,000.00 on eBay.

Dylan had a room in my RV but stayed in town with friends most of the time. Jordan lived in Phoenix. Even though I felt isolated and alone, I tried to put on a brave face for them and support them. I knew Dylan was afraid for me at times. I'm not sure how Jordan felt.

I stayed close to my friends while I processed, accepted, and grieved all the losses. I had some of the most amazing women in my life. They showed up for me as much as they could while I processed. They called, we met for coffee, and they were supportive when I moved into my RV. They kept in touch with me while I struggled with living.

Time moved slowly. I was happy to live near the beauty of mountains, water, and wildlife. Finally, I started to heal.

I cleaned house in real time. I had learned how important it would be to attach, grow in love and belong to myself. I believed I could find happiness if I were successfully connected to my authentic self. It was time to learn how to be happy.

Chapter Thirty-Nine
Happy

While working on happiness, I decided to try to get up and choose to be happy. Happiness seemed like a practice. Like my practice of praying. I thought *it might just be making a choice.* It's *like a visit from a lightning bug. It comes and is felt and goes.* Happiness seemed brief. That was my understanding of it to that point. I decided to set up experiences that supported my feeling of happiness in my life, so I made a list. Live entertainment, time with loved ones, and gardening. I wanted to meet people with similar interests as myself. I bought concert tickets and invited people with whom I had a connection and history. I saw Michael Bublé, Heart, Billy Joel, the Pentatonix, and Oprah. It was a blast. Happy was getting the tickets, time with people I love, and the anticipation.

I want to have a garden. Flowers and vegetables make me happy and are good for the planet. It's one way I can support myself and nature. Years earlier, my mom gave me a book by Mel Bartholomew called *Square Foot Gardening.* The book taught me how to make nutrient-rich dirt, how many seeds of each plant to place in the square foot space, and how to be efficient with water and space. It was a valuable resource. It was simple to follow; I included my children when I first set up a square-foot garden. It was a great family project. I remember I was happy when I finished the planting, saw it thriving, and received food or flowers from it. I was going to have a garden again. I imagined I could apply what I had learned to containers.

Imagine the remarkable healing of the earth and bees if we all have our own organic heritage seed gardens. I would like a space full of bees, birds, dragonflies, vegetables, and flowers.

I have always had a strong connection with animals. I believe in the symbolism of them showing up in my life. Now, I'd attract them to my life and try to care for them. The garden was a wonderful source of happiness.

This was the same year I met an extraordinary friend. I instantly liked her, and it seemed we had a lot in common from the start. Her husband called us "peas in a pod." She was the most fabulous mirror for growth in self-love. I felt a deep kinship with her.

One day, as we were walking up a hiking trail, I was listening to her share about her struggle. I remember thinking, *how can she not see how loveable she is? She is an incredible woman.* Then, over time, her story revealed my own unlovable beliefs about myself. I identified that I was addicted to shame and abandonment, and I felt safe when I was in control. *It's time to get busy, Janna. If I'm going to sustain being happy, I need to love myself. Control is a pesticide for love.*

I started asking myself questions again.

Why don't you love yourself? Did it change? Do you remember a time when you did love yourself? No, I don't ever remember loving myself. Why not? What happened? Why don't you love yourself? What's the evidence here? I kept asking these questions and searching my soul for the answers. I found no evidence that I loved myself.

One day, as I was cleaning, I had this thought. *I was not held and touched by my mother, which impaired my development of self-love. Children develop what they see in their parents. Did my mom love herself? Maybe later in life, but I don't think she did when I was young.* On another occasion, I found some evidence. *I fell in love with dangerous men who didn't have time for me and abandoned me.*

I could see my pattern clearly. Then I asked myself, *why would I put myself around dangerous men?* Then the answer came *because you don't love yourself. Do I believe I can love myself?* I heard an intuitive thought: *you are loveable, Janna.*

I spent 2016 and 2017 learning to trust. The reality of God as love had become my awareness. *If I trust God and believe God loves me, why don't I love myself?* I suddenly accepted and trusted that *I was loveable.* The perspective I had on my "self" shifted.

Once I knew I was loveable, I found it easier to say "no thank you" to people without feeling guilty. I began to let go of the desperate need for boundaries and feel comfortable in structure. I wanted to be in a healthy relationship with a wonderful, healthy, whole partner who would be available to spend time with me. The shame and blame from others didn't wound me. It was observable, and I could choose how I felt and respond. I knew I didn't deserve it. I still recognized the shame and blame and felt hurt, but it was not debilitating. It didn't cut into me. It was an observable action, not a wound that sank into my soul and hid in the darkness. I could evaluate if it had any truth and decide if there was any part I *wanted* to give my attention to. I was able to choose what I focused my inner work on. I could grieve without wanting to die.

I began to have hopes and dreams. I started to build my life for the person I loved. Me.

Chapter Forty
Joyous

It was time for Joy. While focusing on joy from 2019 to 2020, I read many books and articles about joy, and at the end of my time in May, I wrote a daily journal on Facebook every day for a month. It was a gift to learn to look for joy each day. Then, when Facebook reminded me the following year, I read them and remembered the joy again. It was rewarding to learn about joy.

What is joy like for me? I questioned myself.

I experience joy every time I hear a song, and I remember the person I shared the time with at a concert and the feeling of connection and love. Joy is the warm spread of energy inside my body. It's bright yellow, pink, and orange, like the sun, and it leaves a smile on my face. Joy is connecting with other humans, animals, and energy on the planet. It's spending quality time with people I know who love me. It's my ability to love and be loved.

During this year, I participated in a few 5Ks with friends. One of them was on New Year's Eve while it was snowing. It challenged me because of the cold and dark conditions. I felt joy when I completed it, and they gave me a cup of hot chocolate.

On January 28th, Tom's mom, Grandma Fran, crossed over. She had been suffering from Alzheimer's for years. I wasn't in shock and consumed by the grief as I had been with the other losses. I knew I was getting healthier.

In March 2020, I was at work when an e-mail announcement about the impending pandemic arrived. I didn't watch the news much and thought it was an exaggeration. My co-worker expressed to me she believed it was real and felt afraid.

I decided years ago fear is a feeling I would evaluate carefully. I would look at the evidence and then decide how to respond. I believed I had a choice in how I handled fear when it arose. *Is this real, or is it something I imagined? Am I going to change anything? Can I fully trust myself and my Higher Power?*

I knew I had a loving relationship with myself and my Higher Power. The pandemic didn't scare me. The evidence I believed was that I didn't suffer from any other diseases, and I ate vegan. *I know I am healthy, and I trust my body to fight off the virus if I become ill.*

I experienced a calm, level mind and navigated the pandemic without fear. I observed people I love navigate their concerns and worries too.

On April 3, 2020, the mask mandate came out. I was angry.

This is a free country. This sucks. I don't feel free. An inner war raged, but I didn't understand why.

I'd go to the grocery store and shop as quickly as I could, then get to my car and rip off the mask. When I wasn't hot with anger, I'd burst into deep chest-racking sobs.

This feels like grief, but why am I feeling grief?

A loving friend asked me, "Why are you struggling with this so much?" I didn't have a good answer, and then I knew I needed to use the tools I've learned to rely on in my sober life.

How am I going to get to the root of this issue? I need to get clear and develop a process. I can do this. I'll go for a run or a walk to drain my energy. Then, I'll stay in nature so I'm surrounded by my Higher Power's love and light. I can use my breath to calm my mind and be open to hearing my inner voice. If I need to chant, I can do that to quiet my brain, fears, or denial. Then, I'll ask myself the questions and hear the answers.

I had a process I could use now to resolve any issue. I was ready to determine the inner resistance to the mask-wearing mandate. I went for a long walk, and on the way home, I saw a big rock beside the water surrounded by trees.

That would be a great place to sit and ask my calm mind for information.

I took three big, deep breaths. As I exhaled, I thought, *I am safe, I am loved, I am not alone.*

Then I ask myself, *"Why is wearing a mask uncomfortable?"*

My older brother's large, sweaty hands surround my face. He puts his strong arms around mine so they are locked to my body and lifts my feet off the ground. There are no adults around to help or protect me from this abuse. I'm trying to breathe and squirming. He won't let go. I have no control. I open my eyes. My heart is pounding, and I know the mask feels like his fingers across my face. The mask has folds, and I know I need a flat mask that does not lay across my mouth.

I remind myself *I am safe, loved, and not a helpless child anymore.*

I bought a bigger flat mask and a plastic piece that kept it away from my mouth. Then, I began to wear a mask without anger or grief. I could breathe.

When I don't take the time to process triggers, which is denial, I get another opportunity to learn about the trigger again. It will continue to increase in intensity until I understand what I need to do differently. This is how the Universe supports my growth. The question is why is this happening for me? not to me. It wasn't personal. I'm a happier, freer woman and can wear a mask without suffering. My negative energy no longer needs to enter the world.

Asking questions of myself and others is one of my favorite tools. It reminds me I don't know everything and helps me stay out of judgment. It opens the door to learning about and connecting with others, even if we have different beliefs.

On May 23, 2020, we lost our old dog. He could no longer walk. He was a constant companion and a 53-lb furry ball of love. His joy was chasing cats, playing in the snow, and long walks. What an incredible dog. I knew it was time for me to travel when he was gone.

I was free, free from fear, free from others' opinions of me, and free to live in my values with congruency.

My new word will be freedom.

Chapter Forty-One
Freedom

Freedom is the power or right to act, speak, or think as one wants without hindrance or restraint. Yup, freedom during the continued worldwide shutdown. I learned again I'm only responsible for myself. I learned if a person gets sick, blaming another person is inaccurate, shaming, and hurtful. The virus causes people to get sick, not other people.

I also explored my new freedom by traveling as much as I could. I visited new cities and cities I already knew. I went to vegan restaurants and botanical gardens. I was free to be myself, and it was a grand time.

I wanted to spend time getting to know myself in my new perspective of love. I planned trips during challenging anniversaries and birthdays of the loved ones I'd lost. I found my brain had a habit of feeling sorrow on these anniversaries, and I wanted to change the dynamic.

The pandemic meant fewer people and better prices. I was excited. I looked for botanical gardens and people I could visit. I would challenge myself to pack light.

I used the *HappyCow* app to locate places to stay and restaurants to enjoy. I had my GF vegan traveling card for unexpected times when I didn't have a vegan restaurant to go to or was eating out with non-vegan people.

When I went outside of the country, I used Google Translate to make this card with English on one side and the native language on the other side. This card explained what ingredients aren't vegan or gluten-free. I laminated the cards for better durability. I made four at a time, so it wasn't a problem if I lost one and I had an extra to give away. I find them very useful. I have included the template here.

I AM GLUTEN FREE
No wheat, rye, barley, triticale, malt, brewer's yeast
I AM VEGAN
Plant foods only, please
NO MEAT
No mammal, bird, fish, seafood, insects, sauce, broth
NO EGG
No Whites, albumen, yolk
NO DAIRY
No milk, cheese, yogurt, whey, casein, lactose
NO ANIMAL PRODUCTS
gelatin, lard, blood, bone, fat

I often choose Mexican, Thai, and Indian restaurants because they have more options than the Standard American Diet (SAD). However, I didn't know Mexican restaurants sometimes used chicken broth in their Spanish rice and milk in their guacamole until I brought a card.

"The milk keeps the guac lighter for longer," a kind waitress informed me after reading my card in Spanish. This restaurant asked if they could keep the Spanish/English version of the card to post in their kitchen. I always give it to anyone who asks in the hope it will support others.

When I lived in Pennsylvania, I frequently ate at a Thai food restaurant. After making a card, I took it to the restaurant and learned the Thom Ka (coconut soup) had chicken broth and the peanut sauce had hoisin sauce (fish paste). Again, my card was in their language, and they realized more specifically what vegan meant, and it wasn't the same as a vegetarian. I like to believe I changed the understanding of those restaurants for the next vegan patron. When language is accessible, understanding between people is effective. It's a total win-win for all of us.

While traveling in Puerto Vallarta with my son, I found several vegan restaurants on *HappyCow*. The food and the service at these restaurants were terrific.

One of the days, we were in an area I hadn't pre-scouted for vegan restaurants and stumbled on a salad bar restaurant, not listed on *HappyCow*. It was an easy place to eat with tons of options. I asked to talk with the manager and showed her the *HappyCow* app on my phone.

On August 13, 2020, the Camron Peak fire was first reported in Northern Colorado. It's now identified as the largest fire to spread in the state. It burned 208,913 acres and evacuated over 1300 people. Prior to this fire, Colorado had never had a fire burn over 100,000 acres.

My childhood friend is married to a fireman, so as the fire burned closer to the land where my RV was parked, I called my resources. She assured me the chance of it coming to me was low due to the mountain ridges between myself and the fire. I continued to watch the news and joined an alert system. As I watched the information, I learned how dangerous it is for the planet's surface temperature to rise just a few degrees from what it normally would be. I'll refer to this as global warming.

Global warming affects how much water stays on the planet's surface, how hot the air is, and how deep the fires burn into the Earth.

Typically, the ridges would have protected my area. However, because the air temperature was hotter, the fire burned deeper into the Earth, then burned under the ridge and popped up to the surface, on the other side, creating what is called a pop-up. Pop-ups have become a scary part of firefighting.

I was evacuated and went into town to stay with a generous friend. It hurt my heart to be misplaced and still see so much meat consumed all around me. The science is clear that the most significant contributor to global warming and the depletion of the Earth's protective ozone layer is methane gas from livestock properties. When I went to restaurants, grocery stores, and friends' homes, it was hard not to take it personally.

I feel frustrated because I go to great lengths to do my part and be responsible for my health and the planet.

Then I hear my mentor's soft, kind reminder, "Get busy, Janna." I started to write this book again after many months of not writing. I started thinking about a local Veg Fest to attract more veg people to this community and raise consciousness about the health of people, the planet, and animals.

This is one action I can take to grow consciousness around me. I hope someday to help heal the planet, stop animal suffering, and build a community around me. I know the only person I can change is myself, and I know I can take action to find my own solution. I will "get busy" and keep conceptualizing this book, watching documentaries and movies, and showing up for service work.

These are the things that keep me energized and moving. This is how I build a life I love.

I began thinking about all the years of working on myself, creating changes, and trying to become healthy. The words *emotional sobriety* whispered in my ear.

I first heard these words when I was in treatment for my counter dependency. I didn't find emotional sobriety until I was in therapy and reading and exploring my feelings and beliefs. I read books written by thoughtful, emotionally intelligent people. I talked with trustworthy friends. I paused to ask myself important questions and developed a process that created safety, stability, and resilience. I was finally experiencing emotional sobriety in my life.

This is freedom. How would I define emotional sobriety? Emotional sobriety is the ability to feel the full range of my feelings about the past, present, and future. It's knowing what my core values are and living congruently with them. It's loving my whole self and being vulnerable and real with trustworthy people in my life. It's my deep understanding I'm worthy of love and belonging.

I was allowed to move back into my RV a week later. The fire was 100% contained on December 2, 2020. It was controlled on January 12, 2021.

As I moved back into my RV, I began to wonder if my life would be more joyful if I had a partner to share these moments with.

Am I ready? I am ready to find a partner.

My mind, body, and spirit were on a path of mental, physical, and spiritual health. Jordan and Dylan would always need me, but they were both young men building independent lives. I wanted to begin the journey of finding someone to share my life with. I was divorced in 2012, and in the last ten years, I'd worked on root cause issues and identified how my marriage failed and how I had contributed.

I would like a vegan partner.

I joined a vegan dating app. I wrote and rewrote my profile. I saved it in a folder on my computer titled *Kissing Frogs*. I also wrote about the qualities I would like in a partner. Honesty was at the top of my list. Respectful, kind, and loves to travel made the list too. I was on my way.

I meet mostly ghosts, men who weren't physically available to meet or be available in a relationship. I learned what signs to look for, the common story they tell, and how to do some amateur sleuthing on the web.

When my paid membership ended, I was relieved to stop being on the dating app. I met one man I thought had real possibilities. Over the next ten months, we texted and talked, but nothing substantial happened. I learned a lot from this experience, and I knew someday, there would be a partner in my life. I decided to continue to work at loving myself and being attached.

The COVID-19 vaccines were released to the public. I did some research and found out animals had been used to test and develop these vaccines. I made the decision not to be vaccinated.

I was upset by the invention of the label "anti-vaxxers." I'm careful with vaccines. I see how they can help, and I have experienced how they can harm. I was an informed consumer living in America, making decisions for my health. I wasn't upset or angry when people decided to get vaccinated; I was living congruently with my values. I knew if my life required it of me, I might.

Some friends were angry with me, yelling at me in restaurants and calling me "irresponsible" and "insane," texting me long, angry texts about letting unvaccinated people die in hospitals. I was told I wasn't welcome to events I had previously been invited to because I could get an older person sick. I was shamed and blamed by people I thought were my friends. Most of these people apologized to me later.

When did we all stop listening to other views? When did we stop understanding? When did we all become so divided? This is a crisis of understanding and not listening. When did I stop trying to understand people's points of view to avoid feeling afraid, confused, and wrong?

I had very few people in my life with an alternate opinion from my own.

When did I become so narrow-minded? I think I want to change my perspective and remember the year I worked on being open-minded. Maybe my new word will be openhearted.

I stayed connected to my values. I prayed for the willingness to live in a world where I can embrace and love people who think, look, and behave differently from me. One area I thought I could look at was how I felt about people who had supported President Trump.

Have I listened to them? Have I heard what they have to say? I knew I hadn't. I made a commitment to listen and try to understand anyone who was respectful and could explain their thinking on this account to me.

I began to travel. I went to Florida and California to visit friends and family. I continued posting all the best positive parts of my life on Facebook. I realized I wanted people to be in my life, so I needed to be open and communicate my thoughts with others. Facebook was a great way to connect during COVID.

In June, a former student I had interpreted for was graduating from High School and asked me to come to her graduation. I had a wonderful time.

Afterward, I toured Fallingwater, the beautiful house Frank Lloyd Wright built, and the botanical garden in Pittsburgh. My friend from the town I had lived in drove to the Airbnb, and we played for a few days. We reconnected and enjoyed quality time together.

She took a risk and shared her support for Trump with me. I was eager to hear her tell me more. I worked hard to listen to her. I asked her many questions so I could understand. She had some similar experiences with people like mine with the vaccines. I told her about my experiences. We didn't share the same beliefs, but we could understand each other and be kind. I'm so grateful she was willing to be honest and open with me. We bonded in a new way, and I left her with great respect and connection. I now believe that if we are going to heal the world, we must heal our segregation.

I wanted time to think deeply about myself, my life, and what would be next for me. I needed to meditate. That would be my new word. *Meditation.*

Chapter Forty-Two
Meditation

This year, I chose to focus on meditation. I'm still learning about my active mind and how to work with it. I started with a rigid, quiet sitting meditation, and I could only do 10 minutes. There was no quiet in my head. Then I played around with music to distract my thoughts, I added in chanting again, and then I would lay in bed in the morning and allow my thoughts to wander.

I think what I have struggled with the most is having consistency. When I meditated, even for short amounts of time, I felt benefits, but some days, I just didn't want to. I loved myself and gave myself a ton of grace on those days. I meditated when I felt restless, I danced and sang when the meditation wasn't working, and then I tried again. There were days I'd sit in the sun outside and meditate. I had a lot of success with that kind of meditation. A long walking meditation was easy and worked great. No music or audiobook, just my footsteps and heartbeats.

While meditating, I tried to create space. I would imagine a large, empty room. Then, I would pay attention to my thoughts, feelings, and energy. Throughout the day, I would close my eyes and focus on my breathing: *in and out, in and out*. Then, I simply listened for inner thoughts that passed through. When nonproductive thoughts came, I would think, *pass*. When other ideas came to mind, I would ask a question for more understanding.

What I've learned is when I struggle and try to force it, it's hard. Then I don't want to do it again for a while. The message *you failed* in my head can derail me quickly. When I showed myself grace and didn't get too severe and intense, then I enjoyed the ride.

I felt a difference on the inside, an inner calm and security I hadn't had before. I felt less anxiety. My mind was clearer, which helped me stay in the moment more often.

One meditation approach I played with for several weeks was to think of a concept or topic and then just let my mind roll with it. As an American Sign Language interpreter, I have a natural gift for focusing on a topic.

One time I decided to think about my Higher Power Tree. I imagined the trunk, the strength, and the inner trunk of the tree.

The core transports nutrients from the roots to the branches and leaves. This is where trust in God is secured, learning from the past and planning for the future while firmly in the present. This is the part of myself others can most easily see and touch. This is structure and acceptance, which gives my life safety and support. This is where prayer and meditation are practiced daily. This is where my core values are contained.

What are the roots?

The roots are my grounding and support system. They help me see the past, access the water and minerals I need to heal, and become clearer about who I am, how I became this person, what my traits looked like, and how they hurt others. This is where honesty, integrity, and attachment begin. These are intimate and private parts of my life. Only my most intimate relationships can see and access my roots.

What about the tree's canopy?

It's in the future, constantly recycling old and new. Often, these are the things others see more clearly about me than I know about myself. The leaves catch the first chance at the water and are washed clean of the dirt and grime from living. At the same time, I trust the world to care for me with oxygen and carbon dioxide, water, and sunlight. This is the place where I receive the sunlight of the spirit. The sunlight becomes nutrients to flow through me. The exchange of carbon dioxide and oxygen is my breath. The survival traits are pruned and regrow over time into stronger structures. Stubbornness becomes tenaciousness, and judgment becomes curiosity.

When I challenge my thinking or beliefs, processing this information begins in my branches. I'm testing it out with situations in my life. Then, when I know myself in a new and different way, I reveal my true self. Then, the truth becomes a part of my trunk.

When I did this in my meditation, it supported my ability to coach or mentor other women. I talked to them about the Higher Power Tree. I shared my ideas from my life, learning, and self-help work.

When a woman identified she was acting out of codependency, I said, "What would it look like to be in your own container, visualize having boundaries around your roots by seeing your tree in its own beautiful pot. It's important to have a healthy base before trying to help others. The pots may be near each other, and the leaves may brush up against each other, but the trees know where one ends and the other begins."

When a woman identified her behavior as counter dependent, I said, "Imagine you are planted in a grove of trees where you can easily connect with other trees and work together to nurture the soil you're growing in. Imagine you have trust with a few select trees nearby. When all your leaves fall to the ground and become minerals, it's like sharing your pain and joy, which allows us all to grow together and trust others to be there in whatever way they are able. You are there with them, among them. There is no need to control anything. It's happening naturally. Imagine you are all equal, and there is a constant reciprocity of love."

These ideas have helped me through times when I have been struggling. I saw them help other women to understand their codependency and counter dependency, too.

There are lovely YouTube chants and meditations I followed along with while I practiced. The videos had a timer so I could select the duration I wanted. After chanting, I seemed more connected with my body, and my mind was calm. It seemed like it changed my energy level or vibration level. My heart was more open to the moment. My soul was ready to shine.

Is this what functional people experience without all this hard work? I don't know.

Somedays, my mind was loud and needed to be quieted down. On those days, my meditation was more like a loud rock concert. I put on Motley Crew and remembered Tommy Lee on a hoist coming closer to where I was dancing. I focused on the beat of his drums and the song's rhythm. Then I moved to a Phil Collins beat, Billy Joel, Paul McCartney, Indigo Girls, Bonnie Raitt, Eric Clapton, and rounded it out with James Taylor and Shallou. These are the best mediations. My Higher Power loves me. She loves my music, my joy, and all the parts of my brain.

On one of my trips, I decided to go to a group meditation experience. The group was structured with a meaningful reading, a 20-minute meditation, and a discussion. I had looked forward to this meeting for months. I walked quickly to the meeting and found myself in a dark, dingy classroom with a couple of long tables shoved together and random chairs around the mismatched tables. On top of the tables were old books and half-burned candles. There was a small kitchen with a coffee pot toward the back of the room and a hall that went to the bathroom off to the left. A few people were standing near the door and greeted me. I walked to the tables and sat next to a young woman. She said, "Hello, would you be willing to read?"

"Sure," I replied.

She handed me a piece of paper with a laminated cover. I watched as the others slowly came to the table to sit down. As the reading began, I felt my heartbeat calm. Then I read my page. When I was done, the leader said, "Okay, now we will light the candles and turn off the lights for a 20-minute meditation. *This is what I am here for, Woo Hoo.*

I closed my eyes and took a silent deep breath, another, and then a third. I was just beginning to fade into the empty room in my mind when I heard the door open.

Clop, clop, clop, clop. A person was walking toward my seat. EEERRRCCCHHHHH. She pulled a chair towards me.

"ugh," I heard an exasperated breath and the thud of a bag. I cracked open one eye; she was getting settled in.

Okay, Janna, take your three breaths again and go to your big, white, spacious room.

I breathe, 1, 2, 3; *I'm going into my big white, empty room; I see a yoga mat and a candle. Nice.*

"Screwch, screwch, shrewch." I hear the woman opening a wrapper.

My heart starts to pound, and my head starts to feel hot. *What is that? Oh, I am getting irritated. Choose a different feeling. I can't control her, so I can just let go and relax.*

"Mtuh, mtuh, mtuh," I hear her sucking loudly on her candy.

Okay, Janna, try chanting to yourself. Nom yoho renge kyo, Nom yoho renge kyo, Nom yoho renge kyo, Nom yoho renge kyo, Nom yoho renge kyo.

"Crunch, crunch, crunch," I hear her chewing up the treat.

Okay, now she will calm down and quietly meditate like the rest of us. I peek at her and see her eyes are closed. I know she's finally ready.

"Screwch, screwch, shrewch." I hear the woman opening up another wrapper.

What is going on with this woman?! Maybe God sent her to help you today, in this moment.

"Mtuh, mtuh, mtuh," *Right, this is no big deal, it's really kind of funny.*

I opened my eyes and saw her there, sucking on her candy with her eyes closed and a peaceful look on her face. I looked around the room, and everyone had their eyes closed, and they all seemed at peace.

I can let this go; it's no big deal. I can't, don't, control anything outside of myself. I can decide if I want to feel angry, happy, sad, scared, or hurt. Then, I can change my perspective.

I feel a burst of joy, and then, the energy becomes a laugh. I suppress the noise, and my shoulders shake in a silent exuberance. I laugh a silent laugh until it passes.

"Crunch, crunch, crunch." She chews her second piece up.

As I was getting calm in my newfound warm joy, the guy sitting across the table opened his eyes and looked at the woman with a glare. Then he looked at me. I smiled and winked at him, then closed my eyes and meditated in peace and joy.

Through meditation, I learned to hold space for myself while changing behaviors and habits, which allowed me to hold space for others, too. I believe this is grace.

This space is void of criticism. It is acceptance and occurs while being in the moment. As I practiced, these moments began to add together. I felt happier and more joyful longer.

I remembered the space and time my raw friends gave me when I was trying to understand the way they ate. They held space for me to look inside, explore my feelings, experience how my body responded to their organic apple and organic salad, and gain new knowledge. Safe space allows me and others to feel their feelings and express their views and opinions without the need for debate, tension, or disrespect. Space heals our dividedness. As an adult who grew up in an alcoholic home, this is a beautiful experience. This helps me bond with other people in a safe, satisfying way.

Meditation doesn't have to be a struggle in an Ashram. It's running, walking, dancing, playing, singing, AND sitting quietly at the top of a mountain with the sun on my face. It's all the gifts, sunshine to soulshine.

Chapter Forty-Three
Gifts

The other day, I was taking a lunch break from editing, and I was looking out the large dining room window. Suddenly, I saw a tiny set of black, white, and red ears popping up from a small hill. I thought it looked like a tiny cat; then it ran to a location where I could see the whole body.

Oh my god, I think that's a baby fox. I was just editing the story about the foxes on the farm. Is this possible? It's a miracle.

Standing at the window and watching, I counted four baby foxes. I watched them for about 30 minutes in awe and wonder.

Where is their mom or dad?

I started to look more intently at the landscape for the mother or father fox. Suddenly, I saw a black shape on the hill in the distance.

Is that a parent? Sure enough, it was. I grabbed my phone and recorded the kits and the mom watching out for the young ones.

This is a great analogy for me in my life. I am the shadow watching over my kits from a distance. I trust they will be safe and have their fun.

The next day, I saw a full-grown red fox pass in front of my office window.

There goes Tom, my mind declared in amazement.

Today, I am still sober and vegan, one day at a time. I live in an RV, drive a hybrid vehicle, grow a garden, and do everything possible to promote a healthy Earth. I love myself and practice grace, acceptance, and compassion. I have learned from the past, live in the present, and imagine a joyful future.

My sons are the most amazing young men. They are talented and creative. They live their lives in brave and beautiful ways.

My oldest son, Jordan, and his girlfriend have adopted a vegetarian lifestyle with hopes of being vegan. Jordan has sharp intellect and wisdom, and I see him sharing the knowledge of being a vegetarian one person at a time. Like my mom, he is a force.

Dylan, my youngest son, and his girlfriend are also vegetarians. He, too, is a speaker of his truth. He just does it by example. People adore him so much that they just want to be like him. They are the best of Tom and me, and I get the gift of watching their lives unfold. I feel honored and privileged to be their mom. I'm proud of them both.

No person's journey is as black and white as the pages they are described on. I tried to be as honest and accurate about the events of my life and how I remember them as I could. Please keep this in mind while you remember my words. Thank you for reading my story.

Staying sober is possible thanks to 12-step programs, treatment centers, self-help books, and support from mentors, coaches, and friends. Working to become a whole, healthy person and remaining dedicated to the path of recovery isn't easy. I've dedicated myself to becoming healthy, one moment, one day, and one year at a time.

I hope something in my story has touched your life in a meaningful way. I appreciate you spending your time reading my book. **THANK YOU!**

Epilogue

I started drafting my memoir when COVID began, and I was working from my RV remotely. I originally was going to write about my sober journey for the benefit of my boys. We had so many losses of important family members. I wanted them to have information about my life's work and thoughts. As I drafted outlines and then paragraphs, I found myself giving voice to my vegan journey, too. I initially wrote it in these two parts. I asked a friend to do an edit to the ROUGH manuscript. She did, and honestly, I felt defeated. My shame told me to give up. I read some parts to Jordan, and he encouraged me to keep going. He suggested I do some more editing and merge the two parts. I knew he was right. I went back to work and did a huge restructuring.

When this approach was complete, I found a vegan editor and paid her to do an edit. She suggested I format it around the focus word or phrase I had chosen for each year. She believed it would improve the cadence and structure. She was right. I went back to editing again.

The support and feedback I received from family and friends has been incredible. The friends who patiently and willingly heard me read sections were fantastic. I'd read to friends and process deep emotions of grief, sadness, joy, and all kinds of feelings. When I wrote about the people in my life that I love, I read it to them and asked if they approved. Lindy, who wrote the review on the back cover, and Jordan have been my biggest cheerleaders.

I would walk away from it and then get back to it again. I wanted to self-publish and then find a publisher, but mostly, I didn't think I would ever publish it.

One Christmas, while Jordan and I were watching Dylan's dog, he gave me the gift of time. I read the whole book to him. He was a huge support and said, "It's incredible, Mom! I love it. My only suggestion is, can you add more humor?" We laughed about that together because he told me I wasn't funny once. He asked me often over the years, "How's your book going?" and encouraged me to publish it.

While Dylan and I flew home from Ed's Celebration, Dylan read the parts about his life. Then he continued reading to the end. It was a very intimate moment, and I will cherish it forever.

This book opened the door for me to have vulnerable, intimate conversations with so many people I love. It has allowed me to heal some mistakes and empowered me to avoid making some of the same mistakes from my past. I've worked hard to use all the tools I shared in this memoir to keep my soul shining.

On May 21, 2023, Dylan, his girlfriend, my friend, and I were going to the movies. I invited Jordan to meet us there, and Jordan said he had made other plans. While we were walking into the movie, my phone rang from a number I didn't recognize. A woman named Michele left me a message. I had an instinct telling me I needed to hear the message. I stood in the hall outside the theater and heard Michele tell me there had been an accident and Jordan was being taken to the hospital in a neighboring town. We left the movie, and Dylan drove my car. My friend drove her car to meet us at the hospital. On the drive there I knew Jordan was gone. I thought *it's May 21 today.*

Tomorrow is the anniversary of Chad's car accident and Mom's sobriety birthday. I'll know Jordan is gone if they put us in a separate room.

When we arrived at the hospital, they put us in a separate room. I could feel the shock begin to numb my mind and my body. "Dylan," I said. He looked over at me, and I could see the stress and worry on his face.

"Yeah?" he replied.

"They put us in this room because it's not good news." *Pause. Breathe. Let that sink in. Acceptance. Acceptance. Acceptance.*

He had been wearing a helmet, but it didn't have a face shield, and he hit his head below the helmet's brim. On May 22, 2023, the medical team disconnected the machines, and Jordan was declared dead. My beautiful, intelligent, creative, athletic son joined his dad, my grandparents, my parents, Tom's parents, Tom's brother, KC Jones, and all the others we have lost over the years.

Once again, I was in total grief. Jordan and I felt organ donation was important, and I asked for the chance to save lives with the life Tom and I created 25 years ago. Organ donation has been an incredible and rewarding journey, and perhaps that will be what I write about next.

This year, I had wanted to focus on vulnerability, but as I'm grieving, the importance of comfort is what I have focused on instead. I moved into Jordan's rental, and I have the comfort of a bathtub, laundry machines, a garage, and the sounds of the people living on both sides of me. People who knew Jordan. I stay close to Dylan and his girlfriend, my friends who have been at my side through it all, and Jordan's girlfriend.

I have been through a lot in my life. I'm grateful for the things I have learned and the connections to the people around me. A special thanks to my friend Janet, who listened to me read the proof and helped make another edit.

As for publishing my book, well you're reading it, so you know the answer. My prayer is that Jordan is smiling and saying, "You did it, Momma!"

Definitions

Decoding the language and definitions helped me understand the research and information I found while on my journey. The words, language, and interpretations are important to me. While doing my research, I read multiple definitions and then came up with one that fit my personal journey. I encourage you to create your own definitions.

AYURVEDIC DIET

Many scholars consider Ayurveda to be the oldest healing science. In Sanskrit, Ayurveda means "The Science of Life." Ayurvedic knowledge originated in India more than 5,000 years ago and is often called the "Mother of All Healing." It stemmed from the ancient Vedic culture and was taught by accomplished masters to their disciples in an oral tradition for thousands of years. Some of this knowledge was set to print a few thousand years ago, but much of it is inaccessible. The principles of many of the natural healing systems now familiar in the West have their roots in Ayurveda, including Homeopathy and Polarity Therapy.

Some raw, macro, and Ayurveda diets are also vegan; however, that is not always the case.

CODEPENDENCY

An unhealthy reliance on other people to identify how I think and feel.

CONGRUENCY

Congruency is when my thinking, feeling, and behavior align.

Let me give you some examples. My mom said, "I love you," but she didn't hug me. I didn't benefit from knowing what she was thinking, but in my mind, the two were not congruent. As a child, I grew up with so much incongruency that I constantly felt confused and distressed.

Another example is I love and want to protect animals, so I don't eat anything from an animal. My thinking is to protect animals from harm. My feeling is love. My behavior is eating vegan.

I realize with my second example, the perspective of a human who consumes animal flesh might argue that they love animals but believe it is okay to eat them. My response is, please look into animal farming practices, go to a slaughterhouse, then get back to me.

Congruency is a beautiful way to evaluate whether my behavior, a relationship, or an organization is healthy.

Congruency helps me to become clearer when I feel confused. It helps me in relationships because if a person tells me we are friends, but they don't spend time with me, I know we are acquaintances. I take the time to articulate my values before I stop investing in a relationship. I no longer take responsibility or make excuses for another person's actions in our relationship.

COUNTER DEPENDENCY

Complete independence and reliance only on myself. I trust no one and make up black-and-white rules to navigate my life. Isolation and control help me to feel safe.

SARCASM

Sarcasm is defined as a "sneering or cutting remark." Fittingly, the word sarcasm comes from the ancient Greek word *Sarkisian*, which means "to tear flesh." I don't want to tear any flesh.

When I hear myself say something sarcastic, it's a cue I feel uncomfortable or unsafe. Then I pause and take a breath. I try to be brave, vulnerable, and authentic instead of sarcastic.

EMOTIONAL SOBRIETY

My definition of emotional sobriety is the ability to feel the full range of my feelings about the past, present, and future. It's knowing what my core values are and living congruently with them. It's loving my whole self and being vulnerable and real with trustworthy people in my life. It's my deep understanding that I'm worthy of love and belonging.

When I shared at a convention about the topic of emotional sobriety, I did hours of meditation, writing, and rewriting this definition. I have often read this definition to remind myself how far I have come and how much progress I've made.

Feeling the full range of my feelings also means I'm responsible for myself, including my feelings and emotions. For example, if I'm disappointed, I express my feelings appropriately. I maintain respect toward the other person and can explain why I feel disappointed instead of blaming them for my feelings. Taking full responsibility for myself supports my ability to improve inner peace. The only thing ever in my power to change is me. That works out nicely.

FLEXITARIAN

A person who has a primarily vegetarian diet but occasionally eats meat or fish. I hear this term used for the person trying to change into or out of vegetarian or vegan.

I always ask a person using this title for more information because I have heard people use this term as pescatarians and people who occasionally eat meat. I believe this is a vague term, and people use it in whatever way works for them.

LACTO-VEGETARIAN

A person who abstains from eating meat and eggs but eats dairy products.

MACROBIOTIC

Following a diet of whole, pure, prepared foods based on Taoist principles of the balance of yin and yang and the belief that cooked foods allow the body to digest them easily without any added spices.

OVO- VEGETARIAN

This type of vegetarianism allows for consuming eggs but not dairy products. "Ovo" comes from the Latin word for egg.

PESCATARIAN

A person who does not eat meat but does eat fish.

RAW FOODIST OR RAW

Raw foodist, also known as rawist, is the dietary practice of eating only or primarily uncooked and unprocessed foods. Depending on the philosophy or type of lifestyle and results desired, raw food diets may include a selection of fruits, vegetables, nuts, seeds, eggs, fish, meat, and dairy products. The diet may also have simply processed foods, such as various types of sprouted seeds, cheese, and fermented foods, such as yogurts, kefir, kombucha, or sauerkraut, but generally, not foods that have been pasteurized, homogenized, or produced with the use of synthetic pesticides, fertilizers, solvents, or food additives. Nothing heated above 108 - 115 degrees Fahrenheit. The idea is to keep all the nutrients and enzymes unharmed and allow the body the best possible nutrition. Some raw foodists are also vegan.

SECURE ATTACHMENT

A connection with my true inner self, being able to comfort and soothe myself and feeling safe and trusting, belonging to myself. The ability to be intimate and set boundaries in relationships with others. The ability to accept rejection and disappointment in relationships without the need to act out in manipulative or controlling ways.

SHAME BASED

When I was a shame-based person, I didn't love myself or have a secure attachment to myself. I believed I was a bad person. I blamed myself when anything in my life didn't go how I wanted it to. The internal message was, "I am bad" (to the bone).

In therapy, the therapist helped me change my shame into guilt. Then, he helped me resolve my guilty feelings. My healthy internal message is, "I have behaved incongruently with how I believe." A healthy mind can know that a person may sometimes have destructive behaviors, but the person still deserves love, attachment, and belonging.

When I am in a situation where I am shamed directly, or I witness another person being shamed, I'm affected. The shame does not stick to me like a bug on a windshield anymore, but I'm sensitive and have compassion for others. When I witness others being shamed, I'm affected. I know today I can only change myself and my feelings and actions.

TRUE SELF

This is also called the authentic self or the congruent self. This is the me that thinks, feels, and acts in alignment. This self is connected to my Higher Power and has been authentic since childhood. As I heal, this is the me that's attached, whole and who everyone knows.

VEG

The community of people who don't eat meat. Veg means everyone in the non-meat-eating community. It's an all-inclusive term.

VEGAN

A person who doesn't eat any food derived from animals and doesn't use or wear animal products.

VEGETARIAN

A person who does not eat meat and sometimes other animal products, especially for moral, religious, or health reasons.

WHOLE FOODS PLANT-BASED (WFPB)

People who eat plants, fruits, nuts, seeds, and legumes and eat foods as close to how they grow as possible. WFPB people focus on not eating processed and synthetic foods, even though the foods may be vegan, an important distinction. They shop in the produce section of a grocery store.

An excellent example of processed, synthetic food that is vegan is the Oreo cookie. It is vegan, but it does not come from plants, so it is not plant-based. If it comes in a wrapper, it's processed. That is not a whole food.

Amy's is a company that makes vegan pre-made meals. These are plant-based but still processed. They have a wrapper. Therefore Amy's doesn't qualify as a whole food.

Index

Feelings Chart

How do you feel today?

FRUSTRATED	SILLY	LOVING	IMPATIENT	BORED
SAD	AFRAID	PEACEFUL	RELAXED	HUMILIATED
LONELY	SHY	ANGRY	HAPPY	TIRED
CONFUSED	ENERGETIC	DISCOURAGED	CONFIDENT	DEVIOUS
SAFE	UNIQUE	SKEPTICAL	DEPRESSED	GUILTY
OPTIMISTIC	ANNOYED	NERVOUS	SHOCKED	STRESSED

Please leave a review of
THE SOBER VEGAN on Amazon.
Thank you!

www.ingramcontent.com/pod-product-compliance
Lightning Source LLC
LaVergne TN
LVHW051359080426
835508LV00022B/2897